GW01033155

# Inequality and Development

Andrew Reed

UNWIN HYMAN

*To Paddy and Owen*

Published by
UNWIN HYMAN LIMITED
15–17 Broadwick Street
London WIV IFP

First published in 1985 by Bell & Hyman Limited
Reprinted 1988, 1990

**British Library Cataloguing in Publication Data**

Reed, Andrew
Inequality and development.—(Man and environment series)
1. Developing countries—Economic aspects
I. Title    II. Series
330.9172′4      HC59.7

ISBN 0 7135 2370 0

Typeset by MS Filmsetting Limited, Frome, Somerset
Printed in Great Britain by Butler & Tanner Ltd, Frome Somerset

# Contents

# Series preface

Alvin Toffler, in his book *Future Shock*, examined the effects of the increasing pace of change in modern society. The speed of change in modern geographical education to the 16–19 age group is no exception. The methodology of the Quantitative Revolution is commonplace and examination boards have now begun to encompass the more challenging framework of the People-Environment approach and the introduction of value-based learning. In addition, the nature of the traditional sixth form has been changed so that the traditional Advanced level student is not the sole type of student. Sixth form and tertiary colleges teaching large groups and the increasing numbers of students in the 'New Sixth' studying for BEC and similar awards, are common today. In addition, only a small proportion of geographers at 16–19 actually proceed to take the subject in further education.

These contrasting demands have influenced the thinking behind this series of short texts aimed at the modern lower sixth student, ninety per cent of whom will not pursue geography beyond the sixth form. We have assumed that the readers will have taken sixteen-plus geography examinations although the content should present no difficulties for the more mature reader. In all the texts it is our intention that the authors' enthusiasm for the topic, combined with the interest generated by the presentation of the text, will assist a wide range of learners in and out of the classroom.

Every text can be studied in isolation, which should suit the individual curriculum of any group. Therefore, there is little attempt to cross reference texts which might be used in different order by schools and colleges. In addition, a self-standing set of texts leaves topic selection within a syllabus to the teacher's discretion. Nevertheless, the texts will develop new views of the more traditional sections of geography and introduce others where available material at this level is limited.

All the authors have a common concern for the improvement of geography teaching to the 16–19 group as experienced teachers, or lecturers, or examiners. All try to build on existing knowledge of our environment and to stress the dynamic nature of the environment. Where possible, they have asked the reader to express attitudes and explain values towards the major issues which affect our social, economic and physical environment. Above all, the authors are aware of geography's continuing role in teaching people how to think.

David Burtenshaw
Waterlooville 1983

# The geography of inequality and development

Our family routine is fairly typical of many households in Britain. We have a secure home, regular meals and sound health. My wife and I have jobs and our children attend school and college. In the normal course of events, we can look forward to rewarding lives and an old age supported by state welfare services. We see nothing unusual in our standard of living or in the prospects for our children.

When we saw the first film reports of the Ethiopian famine in October, 1984 we found ourselves confronted with the appalling living conditions and life chances of the drought victims. One report showed a family of five who were malnourished and ill, having not eaten for five days. With only a few hours to live, their prospects were frighteningly obvious. To these people our lifestyle would be as preposterous as theirs is to us. Not for the first time we are reminded of the gulf in living standards and well-being between people living in relatively affluent, developed countries, like Britain, and in the poor, less developed countries of the Third World, like Ethiopia.

The aim of this book is to explore the geography of inequality and development. It would be impossible to do justice to the entire subject within the confines of a short book. Consequently, a judicious selection of material has been made in order to focus particularly on the nature and origins of the gap in well-being and wealth between people in the developed countries of the North and the less developed countries of the South. *Inequality and Develop-*ment sets out to identify and explain global patterns of social and economic inequality using a variety of resources and techniques, including case studies and straightforward statistical methods. The main themes of the book are the measurement of development and the use of development indicators, the development gap, explanations of unequal development and a discussion of various strategies for reducing international inequality, with case studies drawn from countries in the Third World.

*Inequality and Development* is designed to be pratical through the inclusion of questions and activities which help reinforce the major ideas and issues described in the text. The study questions provide regular opportunities to monitor progress and ensure a sound grasp of key ideas. The study activities are more general tasks, sometimes requiring additional materials such as would be found in a library. At the end of each chapter there is a conclusion and set of revision questions to help review the work that has been completed.

The preparation of this book owes much to early encouragement from Chris Kington who believed it was possible, to patient support from Caroline Paines who helped to make it possible and to Emily Reed, who helped with the typing. David Burtenshaw kept an editorial eye on the proceedings but the responsibility for what appears in these pages is mine alone.

Andrew Reed

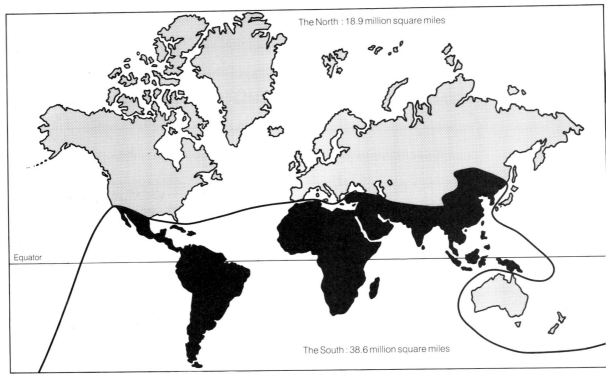

The North : 18.9 million square miles

Equator

The South : 38.6 million square miles

Figure 1.1  World map drawn on Mercator's projection

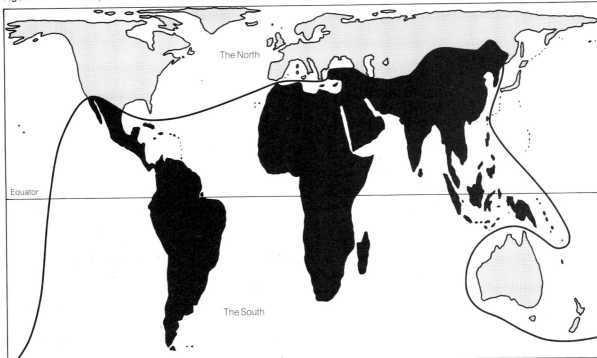

The North

Equator

The South

Figure 1.2  North–South: Peters' map of the world

# 1

# Patterns of global inequality

**Worlds apart**

Planet Earth has been likened to a spaceship which is endlessly in orbit, with a crew that is dependent on the resources carried on board. As these finite or **non-renewable resources** gradually run out, the security and well-being of the spaceship and its inhabitants becomes increasingly uncertain and eventually desparate. So it is with the earth as the insatiable demands of economic man eat into the limited **natural resources** upon which his survival and prosperity depend. But how realistic is this comparison drawn by environmentalist, Barbara Ward? Since the eighteenth century, world development has undergone two profound and yet apparently contradictory changes. The exploitation of natural resources, rapid economic progress and technological improvement have brought material prosperity, transforming the world economy through industrialisation. At the same time, the world's population has multiplied at an explosive rate, outstripping economic progress so that poverty and human deprivation occur today on a previously unknown scale. That the earth has been able to sustain rapid economic growth from the eighteenth century, when the world population stood at one billion people, into the last quarter of the twentieth century, with five times the number of inhabitants, is due in part to the unequal pattern of economic growth. Nine-tenths of the world's wealth is concentrated in the developed, industrialised nations, while the less developed countries have little industry and wealth, and seven-tenths of the popul-

ation. It is also due to the effects of **interdependent development** whereby countries in different parts of the world have come to depend upon each other for natural resources, food supplies and manufactured goods. The main benefits of interdependence have gone to the developed countries because it is these countries, like the United States, that largely control world trade and dominate world industrial production.

In the broadest sense, the accommodation of spaceship earth is unequally divided into two compartments that are worlds apart. A small number of passengers have first class tickets which entitle them to travel in luxury, while the majority of passengers travelling third class will barely survive. This division of wealth and poverty between nations of 'haves' and 'have nots' is the basic dimension of global inequality. It is the result of unequal development over a period of about two hundred years.

**How many worlds?**

In examining patterns of global inequality it is usual to refer to **developed countries (DCs)** and **developing** or **less developed countries (LDCs)** as a means of distinguishing the relatively affluent nations from the less affluent parts of the world. Since the publication of the *Brandt Report* in 1980, the terms **North** and **South** have come into popular usage. 'South' refers to the poor, mainly agricultural countries which were mostly colonies in former times. 'North' consists of the wealthy, mainly industrial countries. Unlike the terms developed and less developed, which have overtones of superiority and inferiority, North and South simply refer to the relative geographical locations of the two worlds. They are represented on a Peters' Projection which provides a more balanced view of the world than the traditional Mercator Projection (Figure 1.1).

The new world map devised by the German historian, Arno Peters, shows all countries in proportion to their actual area and geographical position although there is some distortion in shape. On the traditional world map projection drawn by the Flemish geographer, Gerhardus Mercator, in 1569, the North (18.9 million square miles) appears larger than the South (38.6 million square miles) even though it is half the size (Figure 1.2). No doubt Mercator's map projection suited the European colonial powers not only for navigation, for which it was constructed, but also to portray their dominance over the rest of the world. The Peters' Projection helps to correct this false impression of size.

---

**Study questions**

1 Attempt your own definition of a developed and a less developed country.
2 Why is it more appropriate to represent development on the Peters' Projection rather than the Mercator Projection of the world?

---

Another common way of showing global inequality is to divide the world into major blocs or political areas. The term **Third World** was originally applied to the less affluent, politically non-aligned countries to distinguish them from the rich, capitalist countries of the **First World** and the rather less wealthy, communist countries of the **Second World.** However, as many Third World countries now have strong ties with the major powers, as Cuba and Vietnam have with the Soviet Union, and most South American countries have with the United States, the unifying factor amongst these countries today is poverty rather than non-alignment. Furthermore, the majority of Third World countries share in a common

colonial past in which an early phase of development was largely directed by overseas governments.

Since the 1960s there has been a steady divergence of wealth and development within the Third World which is not taken into account in the two and three world models of global inequality. The most dramatic changes have occurred in the **oil exporting countries** where the discovery and subsequent production of oil for world markets has generated huge amounts of wealth over a short period of time, especially in the Middle East. The wealth per capita in these countries like Kuwait and Saudi Arabia is now greater than in many First World countries, although it is very unevenly distributed among the population and other aspects of development, such as welfare provision, have lagged behind. Elsewhere, some Third World countries, like Brazil and South Korea, have experienced the rapid growth of modern manufacturing industries. These countries are breaking away from the traditional Third World dependence on primary production and are representative of the **newly industrialised countries.** But large parts of the Third World, especially in Africa and Asia, have remained extremely poor and underdeveloped. The United Nations refers to these countries as the **most seriously affected countries**. At the bottom of the development ladder are the **least developed countries**, like Chad and Mali in West Africa, which have few resources and little chance of development without overseas assistance. Compare these categories with the World Bank groups in Figure 1.3. Can you identify the Third World on this map?

It is now more realistic to think of global inequality in terms of five divisions rather than two or three. Table 1.1 shows four alternative models of global inequality based largely on economic and political criteria. A. W. Clausen's eight poles of high economic significance model is notably different from the Five Worlds Models in that it proposes a subdivision of the First and Third Worlds, yet ignores the socialist countries of South East Asia.

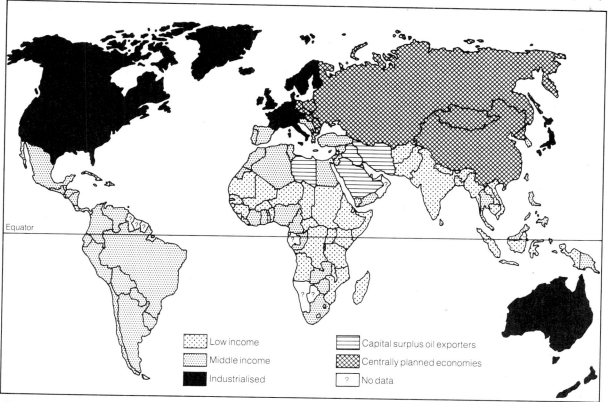

*Figure 1.3* The World Bank groupings of countries, 1981

Legend:
- Low income
- Middle income
- Industrialised
- Capital surplus oil exporters
- Centrally planned economies
- ? No data

Equator

---

**Study activity**

1 In what ways do you consider the spaceship earth analogy to be (a) realistic, and (b) unrealistic?

2 What criteria would you prefer to use to distinguish global patterns of inequality?

3 Explain what is meant by two, three, five and eight world models of global inequality.

4 Why do you think some countries appear in different places in the four models in Table 1.1?

---

## World images and stereotypes

What images do the expressions 'Third World' and 'South' conjure up in your mind? Or, put another way, what impressions might a Nigerian or a Bangladeshi have of Britain or another developed country? The answers will, of course, be very different because what people think about other parts of the world depends very much on their outlook. Their **perception** of other countries is biased towards the kind of culture and development in their own country. Thus a **Eurocentric** view of development is built upon the values, attitudes and experience of development in Europe. A Nigerian would have an **Afrocentric** perception based on the values of his own country. This issue of **cultural relativism** permeates the whole field of development geography and is important in understanding different values and attitudes and approaches to development. Some Third World countries like Tanzania are reviving traditional values and customs as a basis for development rather than attempting to catch up with the developed countries by copying their style of development.

Western images of the Third World are often influenced by popular **stereotypes**, that is, fixed, over-simplified mental images. Table 1.2 indi-

9

cates some Third World stereotypes that have been formed by school children in the USA. In this way, the expression 'Third World' is given meaning by attaching simple labels which may be gross and inaccurate, or perceptive and close to reality.

**Table 1.1 Alternative models of global inequality**

| Five Worlds model | United Nations model | World Bank model | Poles of high economic significance model |
|---|---|---|---|
| *First World* Rich, industrial, capitalist countries, eg USA, Japan | *More developed countries* Relatively rich, industrial, capitalist and socialist countries eg USA, USSR, Japan | *Industrial market economies* Wealthy, capitalist countries with a GNP per capita over $5000 eg UK, West Germany, Japan | *Western Europe North America Japan* |
| *Second World* Moderately rich industrial, socialist countries eg USSR, Poland | *Oil exporting countries* Relatively rich countries, largely dependent on the export of oil eg Saudi Arabia, Libya | *Centrally planned, industrial economies* Industrial, socialist countries with a GNP per capita over $4000 eg USSR, Poland | *Eastern Europe* |
| *Third World* Countries with rapidly increasing wealth based on raw materials or industrial growth eg Saudi Arabia, Brazil | *Newly industrialised countries* Countries with rapidly growing manufacturing industries and increasing wealth eg Brazil, Singapore | *High income, oil exporting countries* Rich oil producing countries with a GNP per capita over $8 500 eg Saudi Arabia, Kuwait | *Capital-surplus oil-exporting countries Newly industrialising nations* 20 countries in Asia and Latin America |
| *Fourth World* Poor, non-industrial countries with few raw materials but gradual economic growth eg Philippines, Malawi | *Most seriously affected countries* Countries with little wealth, industry and large overseas debts (45 countries) eg Ghana, Thailand | *Middle income economies* Oil importing and exporting countries with a GNP per capita between $420–$4 500 eg Indonesia, Brazil | *Great populous countries of Asia* China, India, Indonesia, Bangladesh and Pakistan |
| *Fifth World* Very poor, non-industrial countries with few resources eg Chad, Ethiopia | *Least developed countries* Countries with great poverty, little industry and widespread illiteracy (30 countries) eg Chad, Ethiopia | *Low income economies* The world's poorest countries with GNP per capita under $410 eg Chad, Malawi | *Severely poverty-stricken countries* Sub-Saharan Africa |

1980 data

**Table 1.2 Some Third World stereotypes**

| Perceptive images | Neutral images | False images |
|---|---|---|
| Different languages and customs | Traditional lifestyles | Backward people |
| Widespread malnutrition | Mainly farmers | Uncivilised |
| Unequal distribution of wealth | Primary producers | Living in mud huts |
| Rapidly growing cities | Overpopulated | Run by witch doctors |
| Low life expectancy | High unemployment | Mainly hot jungles |
| Lack of modern industry | Lack of education | Mainly black people |

Stereotypes are a real hindrance in forming objective views on development issues because they represent value-laden judgements, frequently tinged with ethnocentric or even racist attitudes.

**Study activity**

1 What is a Eurocentric view of development? Give an example.
2 Which group of images (Table 1.2) most accurately portrays the Third world? Briefly explain your choice.
3 What do you think are the main sources of Third World stereotypes?
4 Collect newspaper cuttings to illustrate some Third World stereotypes.

## Conclusion

The world as a whole has developed unequally with the most fundamental division occurring between the developed countries of the North and the less developed countries of the South. The term 'Third World' is commonly used to distinguish the relatively poor, non-aligned countries from the capitalist First World and communist Second World. However, it is inaccurate to regard the Third World as a region of uniform poverty and underdevelopment as it is rich in cultural, political and economic diversity. Recent spatial models of global inequality take account of varying patterns of wealth and rates of economic growth, particularly within the Third World, so that a number of sub-groups can be recognised. These models are derived largely from western, and therefore, materialistic concepts of development such as monetary wealth and levels of industrialisation. The process of development in the Third World is often regarded as a matter of 'catching up' in the sense of following in the steps of developed countries, as though western development is a necessary or desirable goal. Some countries are seeking alternative paths and goals to development by building on Third World cultures, values and traditions.

**Revision**

1 What do you understand by the expression 'interdependent development'?
2 In what ways can the Third World be divided up into distinctive groups of countries?
3 How do stereotypes affect the way people in Britain or the USA see the Third World?

# 2

# World development indicators

The publication of reports such as *North–South* in 1980 and its successor *Common Crisis* in 1983 by the Brandt Commission, reflects mounting international concern about global inequality. These reports focus attention on differences between the 'haves' or developed nations in the North and the 'have nots' or less developed countries in the South, and on the ways in which such inequalities may be reduced. Although a global issue, international inequality arises from varying levels and rates of development within individual countries.

## The search for a yardstick

There is no universal yardstick for measuring the unequal pattern of development between countries, since the development process is multi-dimensional. Each component of development has to be assessed or measured separately in order to gauge the levels of both economic and social aspects of development (Figure 2.1). **World development indicators** provide a means of measuring those aspects of development for which data is available and which are, therefore, quantifiable. With stat-istical information on development it is possible to assess levels of development in different countries and to monitor changes over a period of time. Some components of development, particularly **human rights** and **environmental quality**, are not easy to quantify, and although this reduces their utility in measurement exercises, it does not diminish their importance in the development process.

**Study activity**

More than 30 years ago the United Nations pledged itself to uphold human rights and, in 1948, the UN General Assembly adopted the *Universal Declaration of Human Rights*. The document contains thirty articles, the most important of which are listed below.

All human beings are born free and equal in dignity and rights.
Everyone has the right to life, liberty and security of person.
No one shall be held in slavery or servitude.
No one shall be subjected to torture or to cruel, inhuman treatment or punishment.
No one shall be subjected to arbitrary arrest, detention or exile.

The most recent document on human rights came into force in 1976. It lays down standards required of nations in areas such as conditions of work, trade unions, social security, standards of living, freedom of movement and equality before the law.

1 Using evidence from the media (newspapers, TV and radio) show that human rights is a major cause for concern in the world today.
2 Why are human rights issues hard to quantify?

*Figure 2.1  The major components of development*

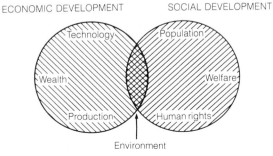

ECONOMIC DEVELOPMENT          SOCIAL DEVELOPMENT

Technology    Population

Wealth    Welfare

Production    Human rights

Environment

## The data base

The responsibility for compiling world development indicators falls to international organisations like the United Nations and World Bank. The data is derived both from national statistics and international surveys. Some caution needs to be exercised in making comparisons between countries as the nature and quality of national statistical systems tend to vary. For example, estimates of wealth in socialist countries are based on different accounting methods from those employed in capitalist countries, while the statistical systems in many less developed countries are still relatively weak. Also, the lack of standardised definitions of what is being measured makes it impossible to assume that every country has adopted the same meaning for particular indicators. Another problem is the extent to which the data covers the whole of a country and its population. In comparing wealth and production data, for example, it is by no means certain that people engaged in the subsistence part of the economy, which accounts for a substantial proportion of employment in the Third World, are counted. Inconsistencies also appear in population data for countries which do not have a complete **vital registration system**. If vital statistics like births and deaths are not registered, then it is only possible to estimate population growth rates and life expectancy data. Furthermore, government statistical departments may be under pressure to adjust their figures to show favourable trends, perhaps to encourage foreign investors or aid donors, thus distorting the statistical profile of their country.

The world development indicators are expressed in a number of standard forms which are shown in Table 2.1. Gross data is not widely used on its own. Usually it is related to other variables, such as the land area or size of population of a country, to give densities and per capita figures which are more useful for comparative purposes. It is important to remember that, at the international scale of enquiry, no account is taken of the distribution within a country, so that wealth, for example, might be concentrated in the hands of a small élite group of people in one part of the country. Clearly development involves not only growth and progress but also the distribution of wealth throughout a country.

A selection of indicators is shown in Table 2.2. Data on 25 aspects of development in 16 countries provides a cross-section of world development in each of the five world regions identified on page 10.

**Table 2.1  Representation of world development indicators**

| Usual method of representation | Description | Examples | India | Australia |
|---|---|---|---|---|
| Gross data | Total size or volume | Population | 684 000 000 | 15 000 000 |
| Per capita data | Gross data divided by total population | GNP per capita (US $) | $194 | $6539 |
| Densities | Gross data divided by area/length of roads/length of railways etc. | Population density | 208 people per km² | 2 people per km² |
| Ratios | Population expressed as a ratio to data | Population per doctor | 3630:1 | 650:1 |
| Percentages | Data is shown as a % of the total figure | Adult literacy rate | 36% | 100% |
| Index numbers | Data is related to a base year or years which = 100 | Index of food production per capita *1969/71 = 100 | 101* | 123* |

**Table 2.2  Selected world development indicators, 1981**

| | Indicator | A Switzerland | B Saudi Arabia | C Canada | D Japan | E UK | F Hungary | G Iraq | H Portugal | I Brazil | J South Korea | K Philippines | L Bolivia | M China | N Tanzania | O India | P Mali |
|---|---|---|---|---|---|---|---|---|---|---|---|---|---|---|---|---|---|
| 1 | GNP per capita (US $) | 16440 | 11260 | 10130 | 9890 | 7920 | 4180 | 3020 | 2370 | 2050 | 1520 | 690 | 570 | 290 | 280 | 240 | 128 |
| 2 | % GDP from agriculture | 6 | 1 | 4 | 5 | 2 | 14 | 7 | 13 | 10 | 20 | 23 | 18 | 31 | 54 | 31 | 45 |
| 3 | % GDP from mining and manufacturing | 40 | 58 | 27 | 32 | 33 | 48 | 63 | 34 | 25 | 30 | 29 | 23 | 47 | 9 | 19 | 7 |
| 4 | % exports of primary products | 9 | 100 | 49 | 4 | 23 | 31 | 100 | 24 | 61 | 11 | 65 | 97 | 51 | 83 | 39 | 99 |
| 5 | % labour force in agriculture | 5 | 61 | 5 | 12 | 2 | 15 | 42 | 24 | 30 | 34 | 46 | 50 | 71 | 83 | 69 | 73 |
| 6 | Value of exports per capita (US $) | 4721 | 11732 | 2889 | 1293 | 1899 | 811 | 820 | 422 | 125 | 452 | 93 | 151 | 18 | 26 | 9 | 12 |
| 7 | Commercial energy consumption per capita (kg/coal equivalent) | 5002 | 1984 | 13164 | 4048 | 5272 | 3797 | 664 | 1443 | 1018 | 1473 | 329 | 447 | 734 | 51 | 194 | 28 |
| 8 | Cement production kg per capita | 666 | 330 | 420 | 742 | 262 | 435 | 378 | 582 | 204 | 397 | 89 | 44 | 78 | 15 | 25 | 3 |
| 9 | % population living in urban areas | 58 | 67 | 80 | 78 | 91 | 54 | 72 | 31 | 68 | 55 | 36 | 33 | 13 | 12 | 22 | 20 |
| 10 | Passenger cars per 1000 population | 34 | 2 | 42 | 20 | 25 | 9 | | | 5 | 8 | 0.9 | 0.8 | n/a | 0.2 | 0.1 | 0.1 |
| 11 | Telephones per 1000 population | 72.7 | 5.3 | 68.6 | 46 | 47.7 | 11.8 | 1.7 | 13.8 | 6.3 | 7.7 | 1.5 | 0.7 | n/a | 0.5 | 0.4 | 0.1 |
| 12 | TV sets per 1000 population | 312 | 38 | 466 | 245 | 394 | 249 | 47 | 122 | 126 | 151 | 21 | 0 | 3.4 | 0.3 | 1 | 0 |
| 13 | Daily newspapers per 1000 population | 395 | 10 | 241 | 569 | 453 | 242 | | 61 | 44 | 136 | 19 | 39 | n/a | 10 | 20 | 3 |
| 14 | Infant mortality per 1000 population | 9 | 114 | 11 | 6 | 12 | 23 | 78 | 35 | 77 | 34 | 55 | 137 | 56 | 103 | 123 | 154 |
| 15 | Life expectancy (years) | 75 | 54 | 74 | 76 | 73 | 71 | 56 | 71 | 63 | 65 | 64 | 50 | 67 | 52 | 52 | 43 |
| 16 | Birth rate per 1000 population | 12 | 44 | 17 | 14 | 14 | 15 | 45 | 18 | 30 | 24 | 34 | 43 | 18 | 46 | 33 | 50 |
| 17 | Death rate per 1000 population | 9 | 14 | 7 | 6 | 12 | 12 | 12 | 10 | 9 | 7 | 7 | 16 | 8 | 15 | 14 | 21 |
| 18 | Natural increase of population (%) | 0.3 | 3.0 | 1.0 | 0.8 | 0.2 | 0.3 | 3.3 | 0.8 | 2.1 | 1.7 | 2.7 | 2.7 | 2.0 | 3.1 | 1.9 | 2.9 |
| 19 | % population under 15 | 23 | 45 | 29 | 24 | 24 | 20 | 48 | 28 | 43 | 40 | 43 | 42 | n/a | 47 | 42 | 46 |
| 20 | Food intake in calories | 3485 | 2624 | 3374 | 2949 | 3336 | 3521 | 2134 | 3076 | 2562 | 2785 | 2189 | 1974 | 2666 | 2063 | 2021 | 2117 |
| 21 | Index of food production* | 115 | 69 | 109 | 93 | 118 | 130 | 90 | 78 | 117 | 130 | 114 | 106 | 116 | 92 | 101 | 88 |
| 22 | % of population with access to safe water | 100 | 84 | 100 | 100 | 100 | 100 | 62 | 65 | 77 | 71 | 43 | 34 | n/a | 39 | 33 | 9 |
| 23 | Population per doctor | 510 | 1700 | 560 | 850 | 750 | 430 | 2190 | 700 | 1700 | 1980 | 2810 | 1850 | 2225 | 17550 | 3630 | 25560 |
| 24 | Population per hospital bed | 87 | 680 | 112 | 94 | 114 | 113 | 498 | 187 | 245 | 636 | 597 | 526 | 508 | 400 | 1254 | 4073 |
| 25 | Adult literacy (% of population) | 99 | 16 | 99 | 99 | 99 | 99 | 20 | 65 | 76 | 93 | 75 | 63 | 66 | 66 | 36 | 9 |

*1969–71 = 100.

## Economic development indicators

Is the country rich or poor? Does it depend upon agriculture or industry? How much energy is consumed? It is answers to questions like these that form the most usual basis for assessing a country's **level of development** although they refer only to economic matters. From the evidence of the Brandt Reports it would be correct to assume that economic differences lie at the heart of global inequality. But it would be a mistake to equate development with economic growth alone, as human and social factors are just as important. The major **economic development indicators** include measures of wealth, the structure of production, exports and employment, and the production and consumption of key commodities.

*Wealth or poverty?* Nothing characterises the gulf between the countries of the North and South more than the unequal distribution of wealth. The relative affluence of the North and the oil exporting countries of the Middle East, and the massive poverty in much of Africa, Asia and Latin America are the most familiar expressions of economic inequality.

**Gross National Product (or GNP)** per capita is used as the summary index of the relative economic prosperity of a country. GNP is the total value of all industries and services produced by resident nationals or transferred to the country from residents living abroad during one year. The earnings of foreign workers and companies which would normally be repatriated, are excluded from the GNP. The total monetary value of goods and services produced within the boundaries of a country, whether domestic or foreign, is known as the **Gross Domestic Product**, or **GDP**. In the case of countries with substantial numbers of foreign workers, like the USA where many migrant Mexicans work, or West Germany with Turkish gastarbeiter, the earnings which these foreign workers send home to relatives would be included in the GNP of Mexico and Turkey but not in their GDP. Accordingly, GNP

rather than GDP is taken as the most suitable indicator of national income or wealth.

*Dependence on primary production* Most developing countries depend upon agriculture, mining and forestry, that is **primary production** to generate wealth rather than on manufacturing industry. The **structure of production** indicates the contribution made by the primary, manufacturing and service sectors of the economy towards GDP. It is represented as a percentage of GDP and provides a shorthand expression of the relative diversity of economic development. For example, the economy of a typical developing country like Ghana in West Africa is undiversified and dependent upon a few major commodities, while a large share of the GDP of a developed country such as Britain comes from a wide range of manufacturing and service industries (Figure 2.2).

The pattern of exports is a useful guide to the degree of economic dependence and diversity. Many less developed countries rely heavily on the export of primary products such as farm commodities and minerals. But, with the notable exception of oil and some dwindling minerals like copper and tin, the value of commodities produced in the Third World is low compared to the price less developed coun-

*Figure 2.2* The origins of GDP in a developed country and a less developed country

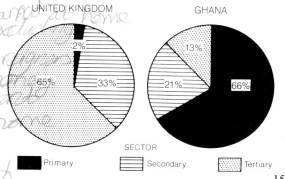

UNITED KINGDOM

2%
65%
33%

GHANA

13%
21%
66%

SECTOR

■ Primary  ▤ Secondary  ▦ Tertiary

**Table 2.3 World tea production, 1981**

|  | Tonnes ('000) | Percentage of world total |
|---|---|---|
| World | 1874 | 100.0 |
| India | 565 | 30.1 |
| China | 368 | 19.6 |
| Sri Lanka | 210 | 11.2 |
| USSR | 135 | 7.2 |
| Indonesia | 109 | 5.8 |
| Japan | 103 | 5.5 |
| Kenya | 91 | 4.8 |
| Turkey | 52 | 2.8 |
| Bangladesh | 40 | 2.1 |
| Malawi | 32 | 1.7 |
| Argentina | 23 | 1.2 |
| Iran | 22 | 1.2 |
| Mozambique | 18 | 1.0 |
| Tanzania | 16 | 0.8 |
| Others | 90 | 5.0 |

tries have to pay for imported manufactured goods. The relatively low value of commodities is due in part to the fact that prices are usually fixed in developed countries like Britain which has, for example, the world's tea and metal exchanges, and also because Third World countries face stiff competition from each other. Tea, for example, is widely grown in Latin America, Africa and Asia (Table 2.3). A large number of developing countries depend upon one product for over half the value of all their exports, especially in Africa which stands out as the most dependent and least diversified continent (Figure 2.3).

**Study activity**

1 Using information from Figure 2.3 list the following countries in order of dependence on one or more exports. Brazil, France, Peru, Zambia, Malaysia, Bolivia.

*Figure 2.3* World dependence and diversity: sources of export incomes

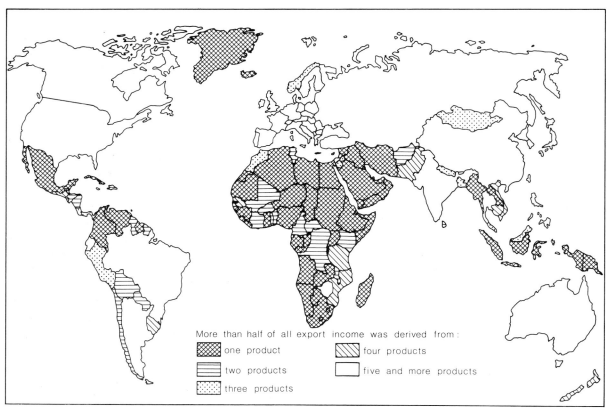

More than half of all export income was derived from:

- [one product]
- [two products]
- [three products]
- [four products]
- [five and more products]

**2** Find out what each of these country's exports are using sources such as the *United Nations Year Book*, the *Statesman's Year Book*, and Pan's *State of the World Atlas*, 2nd ed., 1984.

**3** In 1983 India banned the export of tea. The object of this temporary measure was to stimulate tea production and reduce the price of tea in India. (a) What did this ban do to the price of tea in Britain? (Figure 2.4) (b) How would it effect tea exports from other countries?

1 United Kingdom
2 Jamaica
3 South Korea
4 India
5 Tanzania

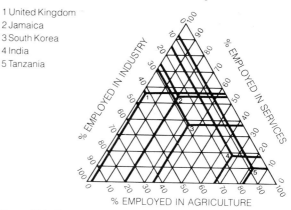

*Figure 2.5*  The structure of employment in five countries

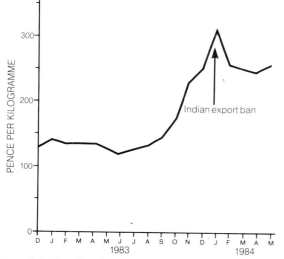

*Figure 2.4*  The price of tea in London, 1983–84

**Study questions**

**1** Explain the meaning of (a) economic development and (b) level of development.

**2** How do you account for the unusual pattern of exports from Saudi Arabia, Iraq, and Mali? Refer to Table 2.2.

**3** Using Figure 2.5, describe and account for the patterns of employment in low income, middle income and developed world countries.

Further evidence of a country's economic make-up may be obtained from employment data which shows the proportion of the working population (15–64 years) engaged in each of the three major branches of economic activity, that is the primary, secondary and tertiary sectors. Most low income countries, like Ghana, have high levels of employment in agriculture, mining and forestry which are primary producing activities. With their greater degree of industrialisation, middle income countries like South Korea have a higher proportion of employment in the secondary or manufacturing sector. Most developed countries and a few developing countries like Jamaica, which depends heavily on tourism, have more people employed in the tertiary or service sector (Figure 2.5).

*Levels of consumption* Wealthy people tend to consume or buy more goods than poor people. The same situation occurs with countries. The pattern of consumption of raw materials and manufactured goods provides a general indication of economic development. The consumption of energy is accepted as being closely related to the level of economic activity, and particularly to the level of industrialisation. The production of commercial energy is costly, so many Third World countries have expanded their industries using labour-intensive rather than energy-intensive methods of production, because surplus labour is usually abundant.

In many ways, consumer durable goods, like cars and televisions, are the hall-mark of an affluent society. They would be regarded as luxuries by most people in the Third World but

17

are commonplace in developed countries. Likewise, patterns of transport and communication systems are associated with economic development. In general the number of cars, television sets, telephones and the volume of rail traffic reflect national variations in wealth and economic activity. The mass consumption of these kinds of product tends to follow or accompany economic prosperity. However, the widespread possession of consumer durable goods does not in itself indicate a high level of economic or industrial development. In this context it is interesting to note the rapid acquisition of so-called luxury goods in countries like Kuwait as a consequence of recent oil-generated wealth. Also, the radio is probably the most world-wide consumer durable and hence one of the most potent arms for revolution in many countries.

---

**Study activity**

1 In what ways are development data unreliable?

2 Draw up arguments for and against the use of GNP per capita as a summary index of economic development.

3 How would you identify a developing country on the basis of economic indicators? Give some examples from Table 2.2.

4 Write your own definitions and give examples of: (a) GNP per capita; (b) primary production; (c) economic dependence; (d) undiversified economies; (e) consumer durable goods.

---

## Social development indicators

For about 40% of the people in the countries of the South, life is a matter of surviving, but only barely, at **subsistence level**. They live mostly in great poverty and hardship, on a knife-edge between hunger and starvation. Global patterns of social inequality reveal stark contrasts in life chances and levels of welfare between affluent and poor nations. In the least developed countries – those with a GNP per capita below $400 a year – the vast majority of people live by subsistence farming, without access to adequate food supplies, safe drinking water,

medical services and educational opportunities. Accordingly they suffer in varying degrees from malnutrition, poor health, high death rates and illiteracy.

In most countries there are substantial variations in living standards between regions and groups of people. In the Third World, great poverty and social deprivation occur jointly, especially in remote or overcrowded parts of the countryside, in urban slums and in the sprawling **shanty towns,** like the favelas of Brazil, that envelop many large cities today. At the same time pockets of élites manage to secure and maintain far higher living standards by virtue of their privileged position in economic or political life. Such affluence for the minority co-exists uneasily with widespread poverty throughout the Third World.

*Matters of life and death* There is no more telling indicator of social development than the chance of survival, particularly at birth. Infants are more at risk than any other age group because of their susceptibility to nutritional and environmental hazards. In the world's least developed countries, the rate of **infant mortality** – infants who die before their first birthday – is high, often over 100 per 1 000 population, compared with a rate of under 20 per 1 000 throughout the developed countries.

**Life expectancy** or the age to which a person can expect to live is also indicative of general levels of social welfare. In most developed countries people can expect to live until they are over 70, but in less developed countries a life span of 40 to 50 years is usual. As a result of improved health services and government efforts, there have been substantial improvements in infant mortality and life expectancy in many less developed countries over the past twenty years (Table 2.4).

The **population explosion** is widely believed to be a serious problem, especially within the Third World. The evidence of demographic data on population change and age structure suggests that few countries now experience high death rates but many developing countries

**Table 2.4 Changing patterns of infant mortality and life expectancy in selected Third World countries**

| Country | Infant mortality per 1000 population | | Life expectancy | |
|---|---|---|---|---|
| | 1960 | 1980 | 1960 | 1980 |
| Brazil | 118 | 77 | 55 | 63 |
| Burma | 158 | 101 | 44 | 54 |
| Chad | 195 | 149 | 35 | 41 |
| Ecuador | 140 | 82 | 51 | 61 |
| Ethiopia | 175 | 146 | 36 | 40 |
| Guinea | 208 | 165 | 35 | 45 |
| India | 165 | 123 | 43 | 52 |
| Jordan | 136 | 69 | 47 | 61 |
| Kenya | 138 | 87 | 41 | 55 |
| Tanzania | 152 | 103 | 42 | 52 |

still have high levels of **fertility** or number of live births (Figure 2.6). With high birth rates and improving chances of surviving infancy, the rate of **natural increase** often exceeds 2.5% in these countries, well above the world average of about 1.7%. Most Third World countries have large numbers of young people in relation to other age groups. To represent this aspect of population structure, the juvenile age group (under 15 years) is shown as a percentage of the total population. Typically around 25% in the developed countries, it exceeds 45% in much of the Third World, imposing a potential and sometimes real burden on social and educational services. The highest levels occur in countries where religion and custom encourage large families, as in Iraq where 48% of the population is under 15 years, and in the poorest countries where large families are often the sole source of economic and social security, as in Mali where the proportion of juveniles is 46%.

**Study questions**

1 Describe what you understand by the term 'population explosion'.
2 Which countries in Table 2.4 do you think are experiencing a population explosion? Give some reasons for your choice.
3 How does the population explosion affect the population structure of Third World countries?
4 How might a large proportion of under 15 year olds within the total population be regarded as (a) a hindrance to development, and (b) a social and economic asset?

*Nutrition and health* Adequate food and reasonable health are basic needs in any society. Most people in developed countries take their food, clean water and health services for granted, especially in countries like Britain. But in many less developed countries such basic needs are assured to only a relatively small proportion of the population. Shortages of food – both seasonal and long-term – and inadequate diets lead to malnutrition and as-

*Figure 2.6 Large families create economic security at home but severe problems for governments trying to provide national health and education services on a small budget*

*Figure 2.7 The trend in food production per capita in Sub-Saharan Africa*

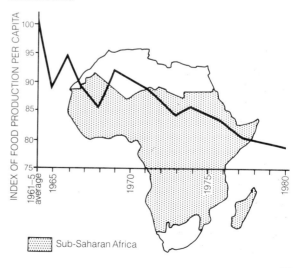

Sub-Saharan Africa

sociated deficiency diseases which are caused by the lack of necessary vitamins and minerals. In the case of diseases like beri-beri and rickets, the cure is simple dietary improvement. The Sahel drought (1968–74) made a severe impact on nutrition and health in parts of Africa, causing widespread starvation and malnutrition. Severe droughts are a recurrent problem in this part of Africa. The Ethiopian Famine (1983–85) has put over three million people at risk and thousands will die from starvation and related food deficiency diseases. Food produc-

tion in the region has fallen by an average of 1.2% a year during the 1970s, and the situation remains critical in the 1980s as readjustment is slow in the devastated areas (Figure 2.7). Evidence of unequal patterns of nutrition is found in statistics of food supplies, data-measured in calories per capita per day. Food production index numbers in Table 2.2, indicate how food production per capita has changed between the base years (1969–71) and 1981.

Another cause of poor health and diseases like cholera is dirty water (Table 2.5). Many

**Table 2.5  Common tropical diseases**

| Main cause | Disease | Main effects | Control/treatment |
|---|---|---|---|
| *Protein deficiency* | Kwashiorkor | Apathy and lack of energy; swollen stomach; skin rashes; deadly if untreated | Feeding with high-protein fluids |
| | Marasmus | Similar to kwashiorkor. More the direct result of starvation | |
| *Vitamin deficiency* | Beri-beri | Wasting and paralysis of limbs; nervous disorder and heart failure in acute cases | Diet with high Vitamin B content |
| | Pellagra | Skin inflammation, diarrhoea and dementia | Well-balanced diet with meat and green vegetables |
| | Avitaminosis | Blindness, especially in children between 6 months and about 4 years of age | Foods rich in Vitamin A such as green vegetables |
| | Nutritional anaemia | Lack of energy, breathlessness; a common cause of death in childbirth | A diet with liver, meat and iron-rich foods |
| | Rickets | Deformities of bones, legs, spine and pelvis | A diet with calcium-rich food and Vitamin D |
| *Water-borne parasites* | Bilharzia | Fever, weakness and death if untreated | Eradication of snails from rivers, canals, ditches |
| | Malaria | Fever, weakness and death in children | Eradication of anopheles mosquito with DDT sprays |
| | Sleeping sickness | Fever and death over a long period of illness | Eradication of tsetse fly |
| | Yellow fever | Sudden fever, aching of limbs and head, jaundice and vomiting; deadly if untreated | Vaccination; eradication of the stegomya mosquito |
| *Lack of hygiene* | Cholera Dysentery | Fever diarrhoea and death in many cases (70% for cholera; 20% for dysentery) | Improved water supplies and sewage disposal |
| | Trachoma | Irritation of the eyes and eventual blindness; over 500 million sufferers | Modern eye drugs; washing in clean water |
| | Yaws | Sores on the skin developing into ulcers | Single dose of penicillin |

people, especially those living in poor, crowded housing conditions, do not have access to safe drinking water, often using the same supply for washing, cooking and drinking. As the level of medical provision is generally low in the Third World, indicated by the scarcity of doctors and hospital beds, few people are able to obtain even basic health care.

*The curtain of ignorance* **Illiteracy** is a major obstacle to development. It means that a person is unable to read and write, and therefore unable to communicate in any way other than by word of mouth. The value of literacy in the development process lies in the spread or diffusion of new ideas. The proportion of adults that are literate provides a measure of basic educational standards within a country. The introduction of literacy schemes, often under the auspices of UNESCO (the United Nations Educational, Scientific and Cultural Organisation), demonstrates the importance attached to education by governments in many less developed countries.

---

**Study questions**

1 Describe the main criteria for measuring global patterns of social inequality.
2 Using examples from Table 2.2, show how developed and less developed countries may be distinguished using the following indicators: infant mortality; life expectancy; malnutrition; illiteracy.
3 Discuss the main trends shown by the data in Table 2.4. How would you explain these changes?

**Study activity**

Draw up a table similar to Table 2.4 but giving data for ten developed countries. Comment on the main differences between the two sets of data. A possible source for this exercise is the *World Development Report*, published by O.U.P. for the World Bank.

---

**What is development?**

It may seem surprising to arrive at such an important question so late in this discussion, but the meaning of development is more readily understood after a consideration of development indicators than before. Development is a very general concept; ask any three experts to say what they mean by 'development' and the likelihood is that you would be given three different definitions. The fact is that development can never be defined to everyone's satisfaction as people hold different views on what is desirable and how particular goals should be achieved. Broadly speaking, ideas on the meaning of development fall into two groups, one based on western ideologies or political beliefs and the other on the idea of development as a process of change and improvement.

**Development as an ideological path**

Several definitions of development embody the idea that the way in which a country progresses along its development path is regulated by its political, economic and social framework, that is, its **political economy**. On the right is the conservative or **capitalist** view of development as economic growth which is determined by market forces and evolutionary change rather than by direct government action. The radical view of development from the political left is based on ideas of **socialism, communism** and revolutionary change. In the centre, and to some extent treading both these paths, are **reformist** ideas of development in which changes are brought about by gradual reform rather than revolution.

The American economist, Walt Rostow, provides a capitalist view of development. According to Rostow, development is economic growth along a continuum from traditional subsistence to modern industrial production. He predicted that all countries would eventually reach a stage of high average incomes and mass consumption which characterises the developed countries today. Even the

21

least developed countries in Africa and Asia, now at the bottom of the continuum, would eventually reach a critical stage of **'take off'** after which rapid economic growth would be more or less automatic.

The capitalist countries of Western Europe and North America have followed this economic path of development. The **capitalist model** or **market economy** was founded on the principles of private ownership, free enterprise, competition, maximising profits and satisfying consumer demand. Under this system the prices of goods are determined by market forces of supply and demand. The capitalist system led to the exploitation of labour and resources both at home and, later, overseas in colonies which supplied many raw materials for industry. The **colonial system** was part of the capitalist model of development. It was largely dismantled by the early 1960s as colonies gained their independence. However, many of the links forged during the colonial period have been maintained by **transnational corporations (TNCs)** and the governments of many developed countries through trade and aid. The process of economic dominance and political influence in independent Third World countries is referred to as **neo-colonialism.**

In the capitalist model, the distinction between public and private involvement in the economy has become increasingly blurred. In several countries, including Britain, the 'invisible hand' of market forces has been partially substituted by the 'guiding hand' of governments as a major influence on development. The nationalisation of industries in some European countries illustrates the move towards greater public ownership and control that is typical of a **mixed economy.**

The path of development in socialist countries such as the Soviet Union and China is quite distinct from the capitalist political economy, being dominated by a **centrally planned** or **command economy.** The socialist approach finds its roots in the writings of the German philosopher, Karl Marx, and the Russian revolutionary leader, V I Lenin. The ulti-

mate form of socialism is known as communism. In communist countries like China, all key sectors in the economy, such as industry, energy and communications, are state owned. In the countryside, agricultural land is collectivised on to state farms and co-operatives, and there is very little private ownership. The supply and prices of goods are generally determined by government edict and not by market forces, hence the term **non-market economies** which is sometimes applied to communist countries.

Apart from securing national goals such as defence, the purpose of socialist development is to reduce inequality between people and regions through the redistribution of wealth. Thus it embraces the idea of **social justice** – reducing poverty, unemployment, illiteracy and social deprivation – and the formation of a more equal society. Several less developed countries such as Angola, Vietnam and Cuba have proclaimed Marxist–Leninist governments and follow socialist approaches to development. These countries form what is termed the **new communist Third World.** They have turned to socialism for its apparent ability to mobilise scarce resources effectively, for its promise of a better society for the underprivileged and its antagonism towards capitalism and neo-colonialism, represented by the unequal distribution of wealth that occurs in many Third World countries.

---

**Study activity** ′

On an outline map of the world show the distribution of socialist (Second World) and new communist Third World countries. Find out how far these two groups of countries, which share similar ideologies, are interdependent.

---

Some of the most interesting views of development have come from within the Third World where perspectives are shaped largely by conditions of poverty and economic dependence on the world's developed countries. In Africa, the idea of development as self-reliance was pioneered in Tanzania following the

Arusha Declaration by President Nyerere in 1967. Nyerere believes that the majority of less developed countries like Tanzania will never achieve rapid economic growth because they are trapped in a world system that is dominated by the developed countries which have a vested interest in maintaining the dependent status of Third World countries in order to control world prices and markets. He therefore set Tanzania on a path of **socialism and self-reliance** to solve the basic problems of under-development without too much outside help.

The reforms that were carried out to create a more equitable society included the nationalisation of large institutions like banks, and the reduction of salaries to highly paid officials in order to cut income differentials in the country. Owing to the importance of agriculture and the widespread poverty amongst Tanzania's mainly rural population, considerable importance was attached to a programme of education and **co-operative village development** known as 'ujamaa', a Swahili word for family. The effect of this approach to development has been to reduce dependence on expensive imports, to expand local industries and to increase self-sufficiency in the countryside, thereby helping to make Tanzania more self-reliant on its own resources.

---

**Study questions**

1 Outline the main characteristics of capitalist and socialist approaches to development.
2 Why has Nyerere of Tanzania adopted a different development strategy from the developed countries of Europe?
3 What is meant by the expressions social justice and the new communist Third World?
4 Using examples, explain the connection between the way a country develops and its political economy.

---

## Development as change and improvement

The adoption of a particular political economy does not guarantee successful development,

whether it is judged in terms of economic growth, social justice or self-reliance. There are problems of poverty, social injustice and regional inequality within capitalist and socialist countries, in spite of the evidence of growing prosperity in many parts of the world from economic indicators like GNP per capita.

With hindsight, it is now evident that the western economic or **modernisation approach** to development has not solved the most serious problems of the Third World such as poverty, hunger, inequality and low standards of living. This failure has opened the way to a new generation of ideas about the meaning of development, and particularly the **basic needs approach**. This was formally adopted by the International Labour Organisation (ILO) at its World Employment Conference in 1976 as a strategy for tackling the fundamental problems of underdevelopment. Basic needs refers to clothing, housing, food, water and sanitation. This concept of development is one of change and improvement, raising the standard of living of the world's poorest people and thereby releasing them from more or less permanent ill-health and malnutrition. The evidence for basic needs development is found in the social and welfare indicators in Table 2.6.

**Table 2.6   Selected indicators of basic needs development**

| Basic need | Indicator |
| --- | --- |
| Health | Life expectancy at birth |
| Education | Rate of adult literacy |
| Food | Calorie supply per capita |
| Water supply | Population with access to safe water |
| Sanitation | Infant mortality per 1000 population |

---

**Study activity**

Using data from Table 2.2, give examples of how the development indicators listed in Table 2.6 may be used to show the lack of basic needs in some Third World countries.

---

A further dimension to the meaning of development as change and improvement is provided by some authorities who believe that the environmental issue is crucial in development, for without a stable habitat, man does not have a safe 'home'. This interpretation, called **ecodevelopment** is as much a response to the issues raised by **overdevelopment** in advanced countries and the world ecology debate, as to the problems of **underdevelopment**. These issues include diminishing finite resources, the destruction of natural ecological systems like the rainforests, the consequences of rapid industrialisation such as pollution, as well as more invidious social ills associated with affluence and western society, including high crime rates and drug addiction. The idea of ecodevelopment is based on principles of environmental protection, resource conservation and human self-reliance. Robert Riddell has outlined what he describes as the macro-principles of ecodevelopment in terms of organisational and material improvements (Table 2.7). According to Riddell, the path of ecodevelopment will require a major shift from the Northern approaches to development, with a new emphasis on economic equity, social improvement and environmental balance. Few would disagree with these principles but the obstacles to ecodevelopment on a world scale are formidable. They apply most readily to local communities where human and environmental improvements may be achieved on a modest scale, as in the case of Tanzania, as well as in China.

---

**Table 2.7  The macro-principles of ecodevelopment**

---

A *Organisational issues:*
Establish the political commitment to ecodevelopment
Remove entrenched corruption and petty bureaucracy
Attain international parity between North and South

B *Material issues:*
Alleviate poverty and hunger
Eradicate disease and misery
Reduce arms and agree to live peacefully
Move closer to self-sufficiency
Clean up urban squalor
Balance human numbers with resources
Conserve renewable and non-renewable resources
Protect the environment

---

**Study questions**

1 What do you understand by the terms 'modernisation' and 'basic needs'?
2 Discuss the problems associated with (a) underdevelopment, and (b) overdevelopment.
3 Outline the main ideas of ecodevelopment. Comment on the advantages this approach to development might have for the Third World.

## Conclusion

The world development indicators are a useful source of statistical information on many aspects of social and economic development. They make it possible to compare patterns of development in different countries with reasonable objectivity, and to trace changes over time. In this context, statistical data is essential for development planning as it allows governments and international agencies like the UN to review the effectiveness of development strategies. It is important, nonetheless, to recognise the limitations of data on development, and to remember that statistics are only as reliable as the sources from which they are collected.

The world development indicators also contribute towards an understanding of the meaning of development through the identification of measurable components of economic and social conditions. But development is more than a catalogue of these conditions. It is also a process of change, influenced by the goals of different societies and governments. Consequently, the meaning of development varies according to different political ideologies.

**Revision**

1 What is the value of world development indicators?
2 Why is development described as a multi-dimensional process?
3 What are the main differences between capitalist, socialist and reformist approaches to development?

# 3

# The development gap

## Gap or continuum?

The gulf in wealth and living standards that distinguishes developed from less developed countries is usually referred to as the **development gap**. It is commonly represented on an international scale as a graph showing trends in wealth over a period of time (Figure 3.1). This graph illustrates a gradual divergence in wealth between the major continental regions of the world. Taking changes in GNP as an indicator of world economic growth there is a more uniform pattern of sustained improvement in the countries of the North than in the South. There are notable exceptions, such as the oil-rich nations, but elsewhere in the Third World there has been a relative decline in economic performance. Look at the evidence of this trend in Table 3.1.

Table 3.1  Changing wealth (GNP) in selected countries, 1960–80 (percentage change)

| High income countries | | Middle income countries | | Low income countries | |
|---|---|---|---|---|---|
| UK | +2.2 | Brazil | +5.1 | Chad | −1.8 |
| Libya | +5.2 | Thailand | +4.7 | Zaire | −0.2 |
| Spain | +4.5 | S Korea | +7.0 | India | +1.4 |
| Australia | +2.7 | Algeria | +3.2 | Tanzania | −0.9 |
| Canada | +3.3 | Malaysia | +4.3 | Afghanistan | +0.3 |

There are, however, critics of the idea of the development gap, like economist Peter Bauer, who believe that there is no clear distinction between the countries of the North and South, arguing that any line drawn between these groups of countries is arbitrary and subjective. Furthermore, there are great differences in wealth and living standards both within developed and less developed countries. Some of the differences can be seen in Figure 3.3. In reality, there is a **continuum of development** in which countries may be arranged according to different criteria. The wealth continuum is shown in Figure 3.2. Notice the absence of a clear division between the countries of the North and South.

### Study activity

1 What evidence is there to support the idea that the development gap between North and South is widening?
2 What conclusions do you draw from the information about changing patterns of wealth in Table 3.1?
3 Summarise the data in Table 3.1 on a bar graph diagram.

Figure 3.1  The development gap

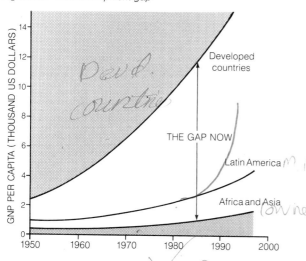

25

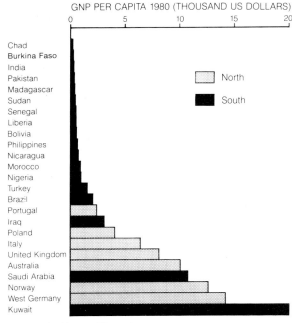

GNP PER CAPITA 1980 (THOUSAND US DOLLARS)

Chad
Burkina Faso
India
Pakistan
Madagascar
Sudan
Senegal
Liberia
Bolivia
Philippines
Nicaragua
Morocco
Nigeria
Turkey
Brazil
Portugal
Iraq
Poland
Italy
United Kingdom
Australia
Saudi Arabia
Norway
West Germany
Kuwait

☐ North
■ South

*Figure 3.2   The wealth continuum*

## Measuring inequality

How unequal is world development? With currently available data it is possible to measure the degree of inequality and therefore to be more precise about the size of the development gap. The data in Table 3.2 shows how the world's wealth and population are shared out between the major economic regions identified by the World Bank (see page 10). Notice that wealth and population are unequally divided between these regions and that they are distributed between them in different ways.

*Figure 3.3   Inequality is often manifest in the quality of housing. This is a suburb in Bombay, India*

**Table 3.2   Percentage distribution of wealth and population by world economic region, 1981**

| Region | Percentage share of GNP | Percentage share of population |
|---|---|---|
| Low income countries | 4.8 | 47.1 |
| Middle income countries | 16.6 | 26.5 |
| High income, oil exporting countries | 1.4 | 0.3 |
| Non-market, industrial countries | 12.4 | 10.7 |
| Market, industrial countries | 64.8 | 15.4 |
| World | 100.0 | 100.0 |

*The Lorenz Curve* These differences can be represented by a graphical device called the **Lorenz Curve** (Figure 3.4). In a perfectly equal situation, each region would have the same share of wealth and population, represented by the diagonal line on the graph. However, the data displays unequal distributions, with, for example, the low income countries possessing under 5% of world GNP and nearly half the population. Projected on to the graph, unequal distribution data follows a curved line, called the Lorenz Curve. The distance between the diagonal line and the Lorenz Curve increases proportionally with inequality. Follow the stages in the construction of the Lorenz Curve (below) in Figure 3.4.

1 Complete a table (Table 3.2) giving percentage distributions of data.
2 Work out the coefficient of advantage of each region by dividing the data in column 1 by the data in column 2.
3 List the regions in descending order of advantage and tabulate the cumulative percentage distribution for both sets of data (Table 3.3).
4 Plot the cumulative percentage data on the graph (Figure 3.4).

The degree of inequality is obtained from the graph by expressing the area between the diagonal line and the Lorenz Curve as a proportion of the whole area below the diagonal line. This value is called the **Gini Coefficient of**

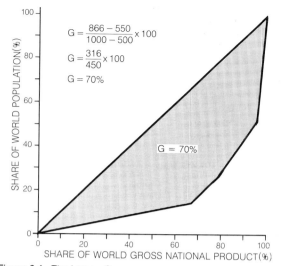

Figure 3.4   *The Lorenz Curve*

**Table 3.3   Data for the construction of the Lorenz Curve (Figure 3.4)**

|  | Coefficient of advantage | Cumulative percentage | |
|---|---|---|---|
|  |  | GNP | Population |
| High income, oil exporting countries | 4.66 | 1.4 | 0.3 |
| Market industrial countries | 4.21 | 66.2 | 15.7 |
| Non-market industrial countries | 1.16 | 78.6 | 26.4 |
| Middle income countries | 0.63 | 95.2 | 52.9 |
| Low income countries | 0.10 | 100.0 | 100.0 |

**Inequality (G)**. It is usually expressed as a percentage where 0 represents perfect equality and 100% indicates total inequality. It is derived from the Lorenz Curve using the following calculation.

$$G = \frac{x - 550}{1000 - 550} \times 100$$

$x$ = the sum of the values at every 10% interval on Lorenz Curve (Figure 3.5)

550 = the sum of the values giving $x$ if the Lorenz Curve corresponds with the diagonal line, ie $10 + 20 + 30 + 40$ etc

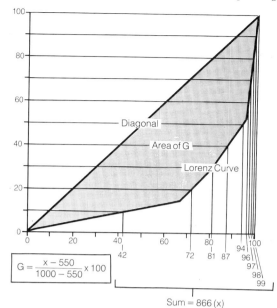

Figure 3.5   *Calculating the Gini Coefficient of Inequality*

1000 = the value of $x$ in condition of total inequality, ie $100\% \times 10$

100 = conversion of G to %

**Study activity**

1 Draw a Lorenz Curve from Table 3.4.
2 Calculate the Gini Coefficient of inequality from your graph.
3 What does the information in Figure 3.4 and your graph tell you about global inequality.

**Table 3.4   Percentage distribution of wealth and population by world economic region, 1955**

| Region | Percentage share of GNP | Percentage share of population |
|---|---|---|
| Low income countries | 8.1 | 44.7 |
| Middle income countries | 12.6 | 23.4 |
| High income, oil-exporting countries | 0.1 | 0.2 |
| Non-market, industrial countries | 8.6 | 12.4 |
| Market, industrial countries | 70.6 | 19.3 |
| World | 100.0 | 100.0 |

**Table 3.5  World development rank of eight selected countries**

|  | Norway | Saudi Arabia | Hungary | Portugal | Bolivia | Indonesia | Sri Lanka | Chad |
|---|---|---|---|---|---|---|---|---|
| GNP per capita | 7 | 12 | 32 | 41 | 80 | 88 | 105 | 122 |
| Energy consumption | 2 | 38 | 27 | 44 | 71 | 85 | 94 | 120 |
| Adult literacy | 4 | 115 | 11 | 53 | 59 | 62 | 39 | 116 |
| Food consumption | 26 | 55 | 8 | 32 | 114 | 76 | 92 | 124 |
| Infant mortality | 4 | 89 | 31 | 41 | 101 | 73 | 45 | 111 |
| Population per doctor | 16 | 53 | 5 | 27 | 57 | 96 | 82 | 120 |

## Assessing levels of development

Few countries progress uniformly across the whole spectrum of development. As a consequence of several interacting factors such as resources, population, historical legacies and planning priorities, there are often considerable variations in the level of economic and social development within a country. These variations within a country's overall level of development show up best using population-standardised data which is **ranked** or put into order of value. The data in Table 3.5 shows the rank position of eight countries out of 125 in the world that have over a million inhabitants.

The extent to which these ranked scores agree or **correlate** can be determined by graphical and mathematical means.

**The development profile** is an effective way of comparing several indicators by means of graphs (Figure 3.6). The relative level of development across a range of indicators can be obtained simply by comparing the graphs. Compare the uneven pattern of development in Sri Lanka, where striking advances have been made in adult literacy and in reduced infant mortality, with the uniformly low level of development in Chad. Another way of using the rank data in Table 3.5 is for a **criterion-referenced** description of development. According to wealth, Norway is near the top of the table, followed by Saudi Arabia and so on. But with population per doctor as the criterion, the order is changed, and the lead is taken by Hungary. This method of analysis clearly shows that the wealthiest countries are not always the most advanced in other respects.

The purpose of correlation is to examine the relationship between sets of data. With a **scatter diagram**, this relationship is plotted graphically (Figure 3.7). In this graph, data has been taken from Table 2.2 on page 14 to show the relationship between GDP derived from agriculture and the labour force in agriculture.

*Figure 3.6* The development profiles of three countries

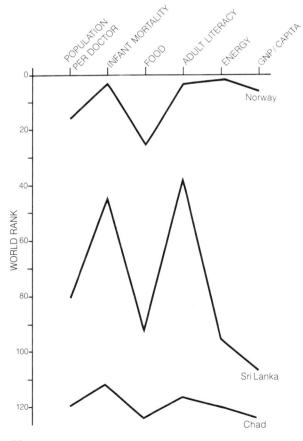

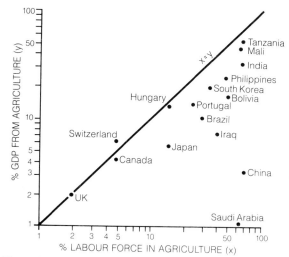

**Figure 3.7** *Scatter diagram showing a positive correlation between two variables*

band or clustering of values. In cases where a high value in one indicator, like GNP, corresponds with a low value in another, such as population per doctor, the cluster of values slopes the reverse way, representing a negative correlation (Figure 3.8). It is important to remember that a strong correlation between two indicators does not mean that there is a strong causal relationship between them.

The graph supports the general supposition that countries like the United Kingdom which derive a small proportion of their GDP from agriculture also have a low level of employment in that sector. The graph paper used in Figures 3.7 and 3.8 is called log–log paper since it has logarithmic scales in both axes. The advantage of this type of scale is that it compresses the upper values and prevents too much congestion of data at the lower end. The degree of correlation is indicated by the width of the

**Study questions**

1 Draw development profiles for Saudi Arabia, Hungary and Indonesia using data from Table 3.5.
2 Comment on the profiles you have drawn and how they compare with the profiles in Figure 3.6.
3 Using a scatter diagram, show the relationship between any one of the following pairs of development indicators:
   (a) GNP per capita and commercial energy consumption per capita;
   (b) infant mortality and food intake;
   (c) passenger cars per capita and TV's per 1000 population.
4 Compare the results of each of these correlations and draw some general conclusions from this evidence.

**Figure 3.8** *Scatter diagram showing a negative correlation*

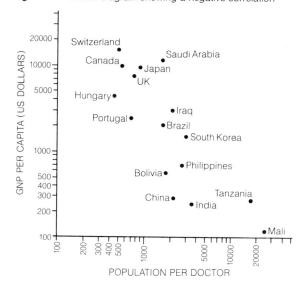

*Spearman's Rank Correlation* To obtain an objective, numerical measure of association between two sets of ranked data it is necessary to calculate the **Coefficient of Correlation** using Spearman's Rank Correlation formula. Follow the worked example below which examines the correlation between GNP per capita and infant mortality (Table 3.6). Notice that the values are ranked according to the level of development which is from high to low in the case of GNP but vice versa for infant mortality where low values represent the most advanced state of development. The formula is

$$r_s = 1 - \frac{6\Sigma D^2}{(n^3 - n)}$$

where $n =$ the number of countries.

**Table 3.6  Data on GNP per capita and infant mortality for worked example of Spearman's Rank Correlation**

| Country | GNP/ capita $x$ | Infant mortality $y$ | $(x-y)$ $d$ | $d^2$ |
|---|---|---|---|---|
| Switzerland | 1 | 2 | 1 | 1 |
| Saudi Arabia | 2 | 13 | 11 | 121 |
| Canada | 3 | 3 | 0 | 0 |
| Japan | 4 | 1 | 3 | 9 |
| United Kingdom | 5 | 4 | 1 | 1 |
| Hungary | 6 | 5 | 1 | 1 |
| Iraq | 7 | 11 | 4 | 16 |
| Portugal | 8 | 7 | 1 | 1 |
| Brazil | 9 | 10 | 1 | 1 |
| South Korea | 10 | 6 | 4 | 16 |
| Philippines | 11 | 8 | 3 | 9 |
| Bolivia | 12 | 15 | 3 | 9 |
| China | 13 | 9 | 4 | 16 |
| Tanzania | 14 | 12 | 2 | 4 |
| India | 15 | 14 | 1 | 1 |
| Mali | 16 | 16 | 0 | 0 |
| | | | | 206 |

$$r_s = 1 - \frac{6 \times 206}{16^3 - 1}$$

$$r_s = 1 - \frac{1236}{4096 - 16}$$

$$r_s = 1 - \frac{1236}{4080}$$

$$r_s = 1 - 0.30$$

$$r_s = 0.70$$

Spearman's Rank correlation formula is designed so that the largest values that can occur are $+1$ and $-1$. If the rank values of $x$ and $y$ were the same then the value of $d$ and $d^2$ would be 0. The result would be a perfect positive or negative correlation. In the worked example, $r_s = 0.70$ which indicates a moderately high positive correlation; ie, the two sets of data display a reasonably close degree of association.

It is possible that the correlation between these sets of data has occurred by chance rather than because it is statistically significant. The probability of the correlation occurring by chance is found out by applying Student's t Test which indicates different **levels of significance**.

The significance or value of $t$ is looked up in tables, or on a graph in this example, to find out the percentage probability of the correlation occurring by chance. The probability levels on the graph are 10% (or a 90% probability of significance), 5% (or a 95% probability of significance), 1% (or a 99% probability of significance) and 0.1% (or 99.9% probability of significance). These levels of significance are generally described as follows:

> 95% level = the correlation is probably significant.
>
> 99% level = the correlation is significant.
>
> 99.9% level = the correlation is highly significant.

Follow the worked example through, referring to the Student's Graph (Figure 3.9) for the level of probability. The value of $t$ (3.8) with 14 degrees of freedom shows that the level of significance lies between 1% and 0.1%. From this information it is possible to say that the findings of the correlation exercise comparing GNP per capita and infant mortality data for

*Figure 3.9  Student's t Graph*

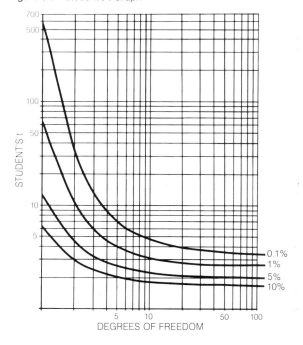

16 countries is significant at the 99% level but is not significant at the 99.9% level. Thus the correlation is described as significant and has not occurred by chance.

$$t = \frac{r_s\sqrt{(N-2)}}{\sqrt{(1-r_s^2)}}$$

$$t = \frac{0.70\sqrt{16-2}}{\sqrt{1-0.518}}$$

$$t = \frac{0.70 \times 3.74}{0.69}$$

$$t = \frac{2.62}{0.69}$$

$$t = 3.8$$

$r_s$ = coefficient of correlation

$N$ = number of scores

$N-2$ = degrees of freedom

---

**Study activity**

1 Using Spearman's Rank Correlation method, test any one of the following hypotheses:
   (a) there is a close relationship between GNP per capita and the value of exports per capita;
   (b) low rates of death are associated with high levels of food intake;
   (c) high levels of dependence on agriculture as a source of wealth are closely related to rapid population growth.
2 Calculate the level of significance of the correlation(s) you have worked out.
3 Compare the results of these exercises. Draw your own conclusions about the relationship between each set of development indicators.

---

## Putting inequality on the map

A major feature of global inequality and the development gap is the distribution or **spatial pattern** of countries at different levels of development. The statistical map is an essential tool in the task of identifying spatial variations in development. The shading or **choropleth technique** clearly reveals global patterns of wealth (Figure 3.10). From this map it is possible to identify the rich countries of the North and the countries with a GNP per capita below $400 which make up the so-called poverty belt of the South. There are, however, limitations to this kind of **single index map** as it provides information about only one indicator, and so should not be taken as a reliable guide to the general level of development.

An alternative method of representing unequal patterns of development is by **map transformation** whereby the scale of the map is proportional to the value of a development indicator, such as world population. The result is a **cartogram** which changes quite dramatically the relative size and shapes of countries and continents (Figure 3.11).

These statistical maps emphasise the nature and extent of unequal development in the world and the gap that exists between countries. They also show that development occurs unevenly over space so that it is difficult to identify a clear distinction between developed and developing countries.

## Composite indicators of development

The idea of combining several indicators into a multiple or **composite index of development** was explored first by the geographer Brian Berry in 1960. His pioneering work consisted of a scientific study of development in which 43 variables were examined using an advanced statistical technique known as **Principal Component Analysis** (Table 3.7). The aim was to identify and differentiate the so-called underdeveloped nations and to suggest answers to simple hypotheses about the characteristics of these countries. The study revealed a contrast between tropical and temperate countries and that many variables were highly correlated with each other. The strongest group of variables consisted of the technical indicators, including transport, trade, energy, GNP and communications, which was considered as a single com-

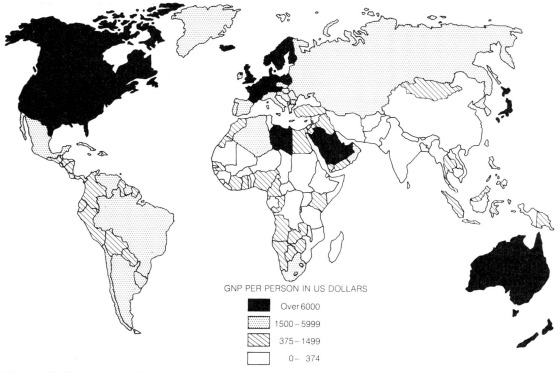

GNP PER PERSON IN US DOLLARS

- Over 6000
- 1500 – 5999
- 375 – 1499
- 0 – 374

*Figure 3.10* World pattern of GNP per capita

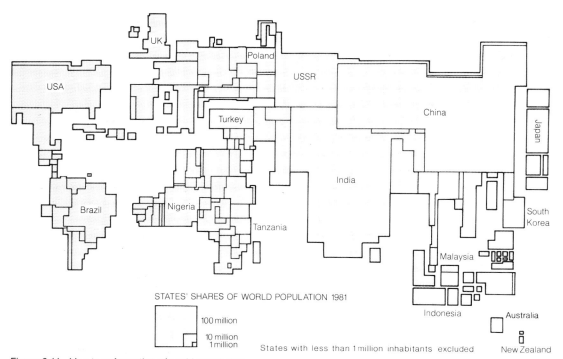

STATES' SHARES OF WORLD POPULATION 1981

100 million
10 million
1 million

States with less than 1 million inhabitants excluded

*Figure 3.11* Map transformation of world population

**Table 3.7 Berry's indices of development, 1960**

I *Transportation*
 1  Kms of railways per unit area
 2  Kms of railways per population unit
 3  Tonne/kms of freight per population unit per year
 4  Tonne/kms of freight per km of railway
 5  Kms of roads per unit area
 6  Kms of roads per population unit
 7  Motor vehicles per population unit
 8  Motor vehicles per km of roads
 9  Motor vehicles per unit area

II *Energy*
16  Kwh of electricity per capita
17  Total kwh of energy consumed
18  Kwh of energy consumption per capita
19  Commercial energy consumed per capita
20  Per cent of total energy commercial
21  Kwh of energy reserves
22  Kwh of energy reserves per capita
23  Per cent of hydroelectric reserves developed
24  Developed hydroelectricity per capita

III *Agricultural yields*
35  Rice yields        36  Wheat yields

IV *Communications and other per capita indices*
25  Fibre consumption per capita

33  Physicians per population unit
26  Petroleum refinery capacity per capita
38  Newspaper circulation per population unit
39  Telephones per population unit
40  Domestic mail flow per capita
41  International mail flow per capita

V *GNP*
42  National product per country
43  National product per capita

VI *Trade*
10  Value of foreign trade turnover
11  Foreign trade turnover per capita
12  Exports per capita        13  Imports per capita
14  Per cent exports to North Atlantic region
15  Per cent exports raw materials

VII *Other*
32  Per cent population in cities 200000 and over
34  Per cent land area cultivated
37  People per unit cultivated land

VIII *Demographic*
27  Population density     28  Crude birth rates
29  Crude death rates      30  Population growth rates
31  Infant mortality rates

ponent of development called the **technological scale**. The second major component, termed the **demographic scale** included population density, birth, death and population growth rates and infant mortality. The third component consists of a group of poor, trading nations which have high per capita trade and mail flows, high population growth rates but low energy consumption and GNP per capita, including parts of Central America, Israel, Hong Kong and Iceland.

Berry concluded that countries were spread evenly along a continuum, with no sharp break or gap to readily distinguish developed from less developed countries (Figure 3.12). In assessing the value of Berry's work it is important to recognise certain weaknesses of this kind of analysis. It is not surprising, for example, that technology emerged as the major index of development given the large number of technical and economic indices and the absence of social welfare indicators in the list of variables.

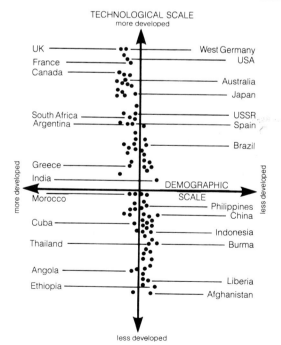

*Figure 3.12   The continuum of development according to technological indices (after Berry)*

Second, the arrangement of countries along a continuum stems partly from the persistence of the original rankings which reduce any gap between countries to a uniform size. Third, the 43 variables were accorded the same weighting, so that significant indicators like GNP per capita counted the same as less important variables like percent of HEP developed.

Any attempt to devise a composite index of development is bound to involve the subjective process of selecting and weighting indicators. At the United Nations Research Institute of Social Development, McGranahan and others constructed a development index based upon 18 **core indicators**. These were finally condensed and turned into a single index which was found to correlate closely with GNP per capita.

---

**Study activity**

1 Work out weighted composite indices of development for the eight countries in Table 3.5.
2 (i) Copy Table 3.9 and complete the scores (rank out of 8), weightings (given) and weighted scores (scores × weighting) for each country. The composite index of development is the sum of the weighted scores. The scores for Norway have been completed to illustrate the method of calculation.
(ii) Repeat the exercise using (a) unweighted scores and (b) your own choice of weightings.

---

(iii) Rank the countries according to the three sets of composite indices of development that you have calculated in 1 and 2.
(iv) Comment on differences in the rankings and the effects of different weightings.
(v) In your view, what is the value of working out a composite index of development? Does it, for example, help you to distinguish developed from less developed countries?

## The least developed countries

The problem of identifying the world's least developed countries provides a practical example of the value of measuring development. The hard-core poverty of people within the Third World is characterised by malnutrition, ignorance and disease. These people, and the countries in which they live, are most in need of **development assistance**, that is, overseas aid, but apart from recognizing the outward human symptoms of underdevelopment, how can these countries be identified?

The special needs of the world's poorest countries were first discussed by the United Nations Conference on Trade and Development (UNCTAD) in 1964 and later, in 1981, at the Paris Conference where attempts were made to define the world's least developed countries prior to adopting a crash development programme to eliminate their common afflictions of poverty, lack of industry and

**Table 3.9  Scores (S), weightings (W) and weighted scores (WS) for eight selected countries**

| Indicator | GNP per capita | | | Energy consumption | | | Adult literacy | | | Food consumption | | | Infant mortality | | | Population per doctor | | | Composite index of development |
|---|---|---|---|---|---|---|---|---|---|---|---|---|---|---|---|---|---|---|---|
| Country | S | W | WS | S | W | WS | S | W | WS | S | W | WS | S | W | WS | S | W | WS | Sum of WS |
| Norway | 1 | 3 | 3 | 1 | 2 | 2 | 1 | 2 | 2 | 2 | 2 | 4 | 1 | 2 | 2 | 2 | 1 | 2 | 15 |
| Saudi Arabia | | 3 | | | 2 | | | 2 | | | 2 | | | 2 | | | 1 | | |
| Hungary | | 3 | | | 2 | | | 2 | | | 2 | | | 2 | | | 1 | | |
| Portugal | | 3 | | | 2 | | | 2 | | | 2 | | | 2 | | | 1 | | |
| Bolivia | | 3 | | | 2 | | | 2 | | | 2 | | | 2 | | | 1 | | |
| Indonesia | | 3 | | | 2 | | | 2 | | | 2 | | | 2 | | | 1 | | |
| Sri Lanka | | 3 | | | 2 | | | 2 | | | 2 | | | 2 | | | 1 | | |
| Chad | | 3 | | | 2 | | | 2 | | | 2 | | | 2 | | | 1 | | |

limited skilled manpower. The question of identifying a category of poorest nations was resolved by applying a combination of at least two out of three criteria: a per capita GDP of less than $100 (1968 values); a manufacturing sector contributing less than 10% towards GDP; and an adult literacy rate under 20%. GDP was applied as a rough and ready guide to the **productive capacity** of the economy and its ability to pay for essential services. The share of manufacturing was supposed to indicate the extent of **structural transformation** away from traditional subsistence agriculture, while adult literacy showed the approximate size of the population available for training in skilled jobs.

The 31 countries that fell into this category are listed in Table 3.8. Africa has the largest concentration of least developed countries, followed by Asia. The least developed countries share not only poverty but basic economic weaknesses that prevent development. As the Brandt Commission put it 'each of them has a slim margin between subsistence and disaster'.

**Study activity**

1 Draw a world map showing the least developed countries of the world. Refer to Table 3.8 for the names of the countries, and use an atlas for their locations.

**Table 3.8 The world's least developed countries in 1981**

| | |
|---|---|
| Afghanistan | Haiti |
| Bangladesh | Laos |
| Benin | Lesotho |
| Bhutan | Malawi |
| Botswana | Maldives |
| Burundi | Mali |
| Burkina Faso | Nepal |
| Cape Verde | Niger |
| Central African Republic | Rwanda |
| Chad | Samoa |
| Comoros | Somalia |
| Democratic Yemen | Sudan |
| Ethiopia | Tanzania |
| Gambia | Uganda |
| Guinea | Yemen |
| Guinea-Bissau | |

2 Comment on the suitability of the development indicators used to identify the least developed countries.

3 Why is it likely that the list of these countries will change in time? Do you think it will become shorter or longer? Give your reasons.

## Conclusion

The study of world development indicators reveals important differences in the relative levels of development between countries. The gap between individual countries of the North and South such as the United Kingdom and Mali can be very wide, but it may also be narrow or difficult to distinguish, as in the case of Portugal and Saudi Arabia. There is no sharp break separating developed from less developed countries so it may be more appropriate to think of a development continuum. At the lower end of the continuum are the world's least developed countries, like Mali, while at the top end are wealthy, developed countries such as the United Kingdom. Any assessment of a country's level of development should be determined by a profile of several key social and economic indicators. The extent to which these indicators tell the same story can be found out by using simple correlation techniques. This kind of analysis provides a reasonably objective method of identifying problem regions such as the least developed countries.

**Revision**

1 Try to distinguish the difference between the idea of the development gap and the development continuum.

2 What is the purpose of correlating several indicators of development?

3 Why is a multiple index of development a more reliable way of assessing levels of development than a single index?

4 What is the practical value of identifying the world's least developed countries?

# 4

# The origins of inequality

The idea of inequality is as old as civilization itself, but only in modern times has it reached global proportions. Over the past 200 years the relatively small economic differences that existed between countries have widened as rich and poor countries drift apart, creating what is called the development gap. In this brief period of history, the world economy was transformed from isolated mainly self-sufficient **subsistence economies** into an **interdependent commercial system** in which the main benefits of economic development have accrued in a few, relatively affluent countries.

**Study activity**

Find some examples of social and regional inequality that occurred in ancient China, Greece or Rome. What were the causes of inequality in these civilizations?

## The historical perspective

Until the eighteenth century the world was less divided by unequal wealth than it is today. Around 1800, an Englishman visiting India would have observed comparable signs of wealth and luxury although some of these, like riding in a howdah on a ceremonial elephant, he might have regarded as somewhat exotic. Indeed Britain was only a little wealthier than India in 1850, but today its GNP per capita is over thirty times as great. India, like Britain and many other countries, possessed adequate resources for rapid development, yet **modern economic growth** which occurred in Europe in

the nineteenth century was denied to India and the majority of countries in Africa, Asia and Latin America.

The search for the origins of inequality starts, therefore, in Europe, and especially in Britain where the seeds of modern affluence were sown. From there, modern economic development spread quickly to the New World and Japan. The rest of the world remained relatively poor and backward. So the search for an explanation of inequality continues with an examination of the **barriers to development** in the Third World. Finally in this chapter, some **explanatory models** of development are considered to provide a theoretical framework to an understanding of global inequality.

## The cradle of affluence

Britain was the first country in the world to experience modern economic growth. It was achieved largely as the result of technical improvements which first transformed the cotton manufacturing process and subsequently the production of iron and steel during a period of intense and unprecedented social and economic changes referred to as the **industrial revolution** (Table 4.1).

The progress of **economic transformation** was slow at first but accelerated during the nineteenth century as coal replaced water and human labour as the main sources of power in factories, and as more sophisticated machines gradually replaced the relatively simple technology of the early phase of the industrial revolution. Britain had reached the stage of

**Table 4.1   Some major inventions and technical achievements, 1700–1850**

| Inventor | Invention | Date | Place |
|---|---|---|---|
| Thomas Newcomen | Earliest steam engine used in Cornish tin mines | 1705 | England |
| John Kay | The flying shuttle revolutionized cotton weaving and ousted the traditional hand-loom | 1733 | England |
| James Hargreaves | The spinning jenny enabled one spinner to spin several threads at once | 1764 | England |
| Richard Arkwright | The spinning frame was powered by water | 1769 | England |
| Samuel Crompton | The spinning mule combined rollers and spindles in a single machine | 1779 | England |
| Abraham Darby | Built the first cast-iron bridge | 1779 | England |
| Edmund Cartwright | Applied steam power to the loom | 1785 | England |
| James Watt | Improved the steam engine | 1785 | Scotland |
| George Stephenson | Built the first locomotive for public use | 1825 | England |
| Samuel Morse | Pioneer of electromagnetic telegraphy | 1832 | USA |
| Henry Bessemer | Revolutionised the production of steel from cast-iron in a single process | 1850 | England |

**economic take-off** when further growth seemed assured. With the coming of the railway, **industrialisation** spread rapidly as materials and products could be exchanged more easily between regions and isolated centres of manufacturing and population. The railway network, started in 1825 between Stockton and Darlington, was virtually complete by 1850. With the arrival of the railway age, Britain emerged as a fully industrialised nation producing more goods and transporting them more rapidly than any other country in the world (Figure 4.1). The effect on society was profound as the accompanying process of **urbanisation** led to the building of extensive areas of housing and factories and the emergence of six giant **conurbations** which, by 1881, accounted for 40% of the population of England and Wales. The industrial revolution had turned Britain into an urban society with values and attitudes rooted in the new **urban-industrial environment** of the city. Although standards of living may have declined in the early stage of the industrial revolution, after 1870 the spread of wealth, improved eating habits and diets, better public health provision and housing helped to bring about a steady improvement. The rate of infant mortality fell from around 150 per 1 000 in 1850 to about 105 per 1 000 in 1914. The **medical revolution** ensured the downward trend in mortality rates, with discoveries like vaccination against smallpox (Jenner, 1798), immunisation against germs (Pasteur, *c* 1880), antiseptic surgery (Lister, 1865) and penicillin (Fleming, 1928).

*Figure 4.1   British industrial output as a percentage of world total, 1780–1960*

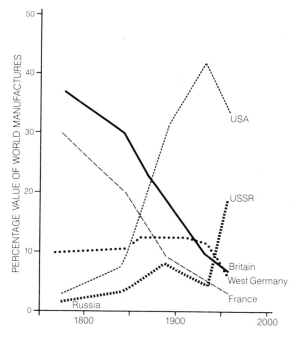

**Study questions**

1 What was the nature and duration of the industrial revolution?

2 To what extent is it possible to identify different phases of development during the industrial revolution?

3 Discuss the role of each of the following in the evolution of modern industrial society in Britain: (a) technological change; (b) railways; (c) urbanisation.

4 How far would you agree that modern economic growth during the industrial revolution was evolutionary rather than revolutionary?

5 Comment on the main trends in industrial output shown on the graph in Figure 4.1.

### The diffusion of modern economic growth

From Britain, modern economic development spread to Belgium and then the rest of Europe. It occurred in Germany after unification in 1871 and more slowly in France, where, in spite of the revolution in 1789, traditional social values and conservatism held back rapid growth until the early twentieth century. Russian development was stifled initially by a feudal society and inadequate infrastructure. However, following the 1917 revolution it set the pattern for centrally planned economic growth through a series of Five Year Plans which stressed the development of heavy industry. The countries of the New World industrialised rapidly following the waves of immigrant settlers from Europe during the nineteenth century. The only non-European country to modernise its economy at this time was Japan which opened its doors to western influence after the restoration of the Meiji Emperor in 1868 and the rejection of the feudal regime which had previously protected Japan from foreign contact and trade through the Seclusion Edicts. Some developing countries have experienced economic take off, but in many cases such as India, progress is hampered by rapid population growth. Rostow's **stages of economic growth model**, dating from 1960, indicates the relative timing of modern economic growth from the initial phase of industrial take off to a stage of economic

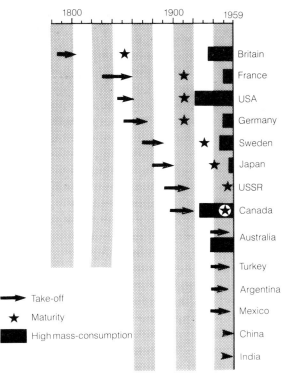

**Figure 4.2** *Rostow's timing of economic growth in selected countries, 1960*

maturity (Figure 4.2). The stages are discussed in detail on page 55.

**Study questions**

1 Explain the timing of economic take-off and maturity for the countries shown in Figure 4.2.

2 Why do you think it is difficult to be precise about the timing of economic take-off?

3 Rostow's main criteria for economic take-off was for a country to achieve a level of national savings not less than 10% of its national income, that is the monetary value of all goods and services produced in an economy. What are the strengths and weaknesses of this criterion?

### Revolution or evolution?

The forces that brought Britain rather than any other country to the Industrial Revolution were evolutionary rather than revolutionary. They demonstrate the importance of **pre-**

**conditions for industrial take-off** and the reasons why Britain was able to break down the barriers to modern economic growth at that time. Britain was relatively affluent in the mid-eighteenth century. British farms were efficient and progressive as landowners made enclosures and sought improved farming methods. There was also a well-established manufacturing sector employing skilled craftsmen or **artisan** workers and coal was mined for urban fireplaces well before its appearance in industry. The growing population, doubling itself every fifty years, stimulated demand for farm and factory goods, and provided an abundant supply of cheap labour for industry. But it was chiefly **trade** that brought wealth to Britain before the Industrial Revolution. British foreign policy was subordinated to economic ends through the acquisition of **colonies** for raw materials and markets. The passing of the Navigation Act in 1651, described by eighteenth century economist Adam Smith in his book the *Wealth of Nations* as 'perhaps the wisest of all commercial regulations in England', led to the virtual monopoly of colonial trade by British shipping and merchants until the mid-nineteenth century. This **commercial revolution** saw the rise of the East India Company and the rapid expansion of the Indian and Far Eastern trade and the inhuman but lucrative slave traffic between Africa and the colonies in North America and the Caribbean. The profits of merchants, shipowners and manufacturers accumulated as vital **capital** in London and other commercial cities, providing the springboard for subsequent investment and economic growth. The effectiveness of this wealth was in part due to British **entrepreneurship** whereby individuals or firms invested their capital profitably in businesses and industries.

> **Study questions**
>
> 1 Explain why the Industrial Revolution was, in fact, evolutionary.
> 2 Summarise the pre-conditions for industrialisation in Britain.
> 3 Entrepreneurs have been described as decision-makers and risk-takers. Can you think of any reasons for this?
> 4 What was the main role of the colonies in the economic development of Britain?

### Barriers to economic development

It is unlikely that any single barrier has seriously hampered economic development in the Third World. The experience of most low income countries indicates that underdevelopment and the persistence of traditional subsistence economies are associated with a range of obstacles to progress. Some obstacles, like droughts, are relatively **short-term barriers** and usually localised. Others, like dependence on primary products, are **long-term or structural barriers** which can only be overcome by major changes or reforms. The extent to which a country can overcome barriers to economic development depends largely on whether they are **internal barriers**, such as environmental conditions, over which a country has some influence or **external barriers**, like world commodity prices, which are beyond the control of a single country. The most formidable barriers are both economic and non-economic, including adverse environmental conditions, the impact of colonialism, shortages of capital, institutional bottlenecks and the population explosion.

*Harsh environments* The Third World lies mainly in the tropics where **environmental systems** are generally fragile and easily destabilised by inappropriate farming practices and deforestation or rapid population growth. The ecological disaster facing the small African state of Burundi demonstrates the onset of **ecological imbalance** which to some extent affects most Third World countries (Figure 4.3).

The most widespread environmental barrier to rural development is the lack of water that characterises most tropical regions. Many

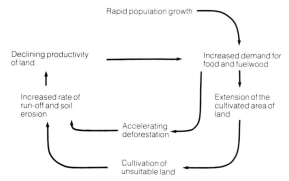

*Figure 4.3* The cycle of ecological imbalance

parts of the Third World experience low annual rainfall or seasonal rainfall, like the monsoon regime of south and south-east Asia and the tropical grassland region of Africa. Unreliable and unpredictable rainfall in India leads to regular occurrences of droughts and floods. The problem is particularly severe in the densely populated plains of the Ganges in states like Bihar and West Bengal, and in the Deccan Plateau region of peninsular India where there is little perennial (all year) irrigation. The regular loss or depletion of harvests by bad weather helps spread **rural poverty** as farmers lose their incomes and means of livelihood. Apart from the loss of life, there are the economic consequences of devastated crops, fields and buildings and disrupted communications that follow in the wake of natural disasters. The monsoon floods of Rajasthan in 1979 killed an estimated 1000 people and 4000 head of cattle, left thousands of people homeless and ruined 300000 hectares of cropped land.

Occasionally droughts can have catastrophic long-term effects on economic development as in the case of the Sahel region of Africa which stretches along the southern edge of the Sahara Desert (Figure 4.4). The prolonged drought of the early 1970s and 1980s and the rapid deple-

*Figure 4.4* World distribution of deserts and desertification

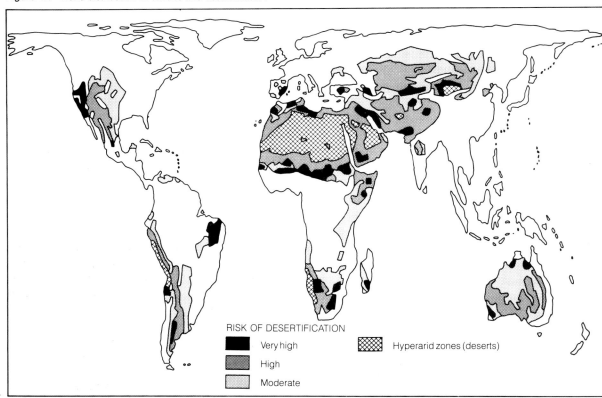

RISK OF DESERTIFICATION

- Very high
- High
- Moderate
- Hyperarid zones (deserts)

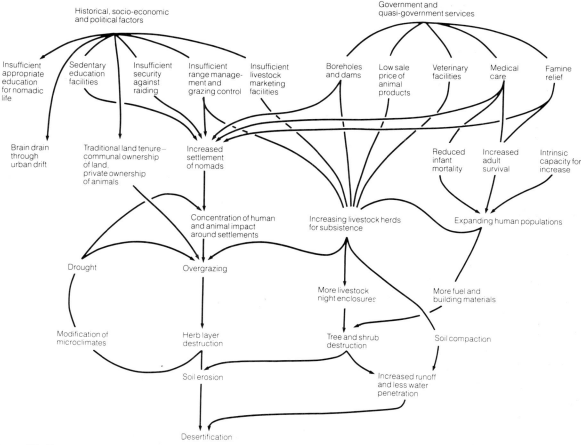

**Figure 4.5** *The main causes of desertification in northern Kenya
(after H Lamprey)*

tion of the tropical pastures of the Sahel by nomadic herdsmen, such as the Tuareg, led to soil erosion and the gradual advance of desert conditions into the savanna grasslands. Figure 4.5 shows the causes of desert encroachment in northern Kenya. This process, known as **desertification**, has caused great social and economic problems for the people of the Sahel by reducing the amount of economically productive land and means of subsistence in the region at a time of rapid population growth. Development efforts in the Sahel are now being directed towards long-term solutions but the cost of major reclamation, irrigation and resettlement schemes is beyond the means of local governments. So Sahelian countries like Burkina Faso and Ethiopia are forced to seek overseas assistance and become heavily dependent upon **foreign aid**.

**Study activity**

Find out all you can about the effects of drought in (a) north-east Brazil and (b) Ethiopia, and the measures the respective governments are taking to find long-term solutions to the drought problem of these countries.

**Study questions**

1 Describe the differences between internal and external barriers to development.

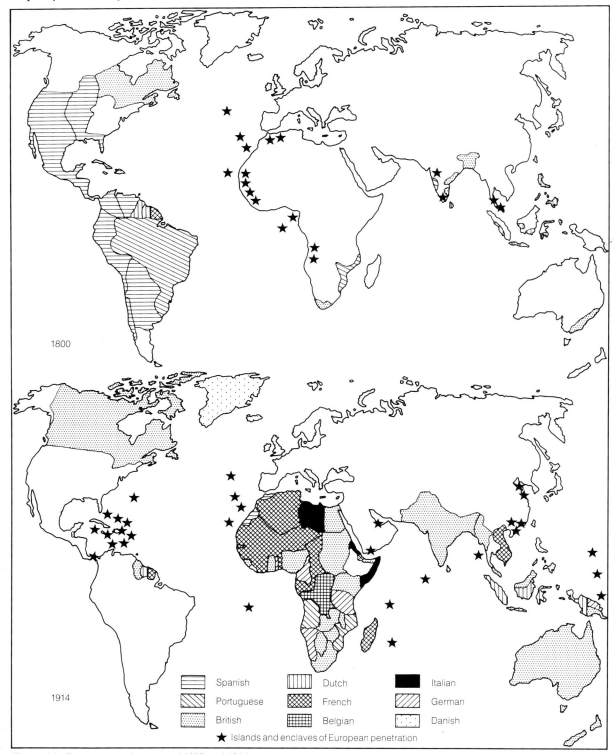

**Figure 4.6** *European empires around 1800 and 1914*

2 Explain the meaning of the terms 'ecological imbalance' and 'desertification'.

3 Account for the spread of desert conditions in northern Kenya. Refer to Figure 4.5.

4 Discuss the long-term consequences of the Sahelian drought for development in the region.

*The impact of colonialism* The expansion of European influence through the acquisition of colonies had a profound impact upon global patterns of development. Europe and its possessions overseas had occupied at some time during the colonial era (1450–1960) some 85% of the world's territory (Figure 4.6). During this period many of the largely undiscovered and underdeveloped regions of Latin America, Africa and Asia were explored, exploited and annexed, to meet the economic requirements of the imperial powers. These regions were drawn into the world economic system not as equal partners but as **dependent territories**. Within this general political and economic framework, the effects of colonialism on economic development in the Third World have varied widely according to the motives and actions of the colonizing powers and the geographical conditions within the colonies.

The first phase of European domination was in Latin America between 1450 and 1800 when the Spanish and Portuguese, in particular, were motivated by economic gain – especially for supplies of gold and silver. But in addition to mining, the European settlers introduced a **plantation system** to grow tropical products such as coffee, rubber and bananas for export, using cheap slave labour. The colonial development of Latin America was exploitive, entailing the extraction of resources and the virtual extinction of indigenous populations like the Incas of Peru. The economic benefits of development went to Europe and the European settlers. After **independence** in the early nineteenth century, Latin American countries continued to remain economically dependent on markets in Europe. With the opening up of Africa they lost their monopoly over the supply of precious metals and tropical produce, and became increasingly vulnerable to competition and fluctuating prices.

The second major phase of European expansion took place between about 1750 and 1945. It was largely ordained by the industrial revolution and the growing demand for raw materials. The principal targets were Africa and Asia. The scramble for Africa led to the partition of the entire continent by Britain, France, Portugal and several other European countries. The main economic result was the establishment of commercial agriculture, for export crops, either on plantations which the French encouraged or on smallholdings which were typical of the British West African colonies (Figure 4.8). The introduction of **cash crops** into the subsistence economy tended to lure farmers away from full-time food production, as in Ghana and Nigeria (Figure 4.7). Elsewhere, pastoralists and nomads were dispossessed of the traditional grazing lands in favour of cotton, groundnuts and other cash crops. In Kenya, African pastoralists and farmers, like the nomadic Masai and the settled Kikuyu, were restricted to native **reserves** outside the fertile White Highlands which became parcelled out for European farmers. In South Africa, **rural reserve policies** laid the found-

*Figure 4.7 The message in Ghana's food campaign is clear. Like many Third World countries, Ghana has concentrated on the production of export crops at the expense of growing food for home consumption*

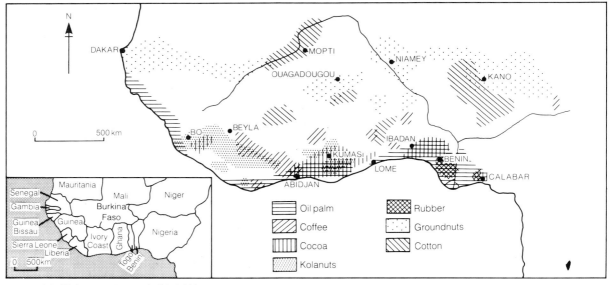

*Figure 4.8* Major export crops in West Africa

ations for separate or **apartheid** development for black Africans and Whites, and the pattern of migrant labour between tribal areas and European-owned gold and diamond mines in the Rand and at Kimberley. The resources of the colonial administrators were concentrated in the development of cash crops and mining, and in the construction of the roads, railways and port facilities that were necessary for the successful commercial exploitation of the colonies. In certain areas the expansion of cash cropping and mining led to the neglect of food production. The emphasis on groundnut production in Senegal forced many farmers to rely on imported supplies of rice. Senegal and other African countries now spend large sums of hard-earned **foreign exchange** on imported food supplies which could be grown much more cheaply at home (Table 4.2). The **monoculture system** of single crop production on plantations also had long-term adverse effects. The impoverished soils of Mali, Burkina Faso and Niger are due largely to the prolonged cultivation of cotton in the colonial period.

The second phase of colonialism also took the European powers to Asia. The Dutch controlled Indonesia, or the Dutch East Indies

**Table 4.2  Senegal's foreign trade, 1980 (in US million $)**

|  | Imports | Exports |
| --- | --- | --- |
| Food, animals and drink | 22.6 | 34.0 |
| Raw materials | 3.7 | 34.1 |
| Oil | 19.5 | 17.5 |
| Chemicals | 8.5 | 5.1 |
| Manufactured goods | 20.1 | 5.8 |
| Machinery and transport equipment | 25.6 | 3.5 |

as it was called, and Java came under the **culture system** which forced Javanese farmers to use a fifth of their land for growing cash crops like sugar, tea and coffee and other foodstuffs for export to the Netherlands. In this way Java's subsistence economy was transformed into a dependent economy and rural poverty spread as peasant farmers were exploited in the cultivation of cash crops. Malaya became dependent upon the British economy following the successful introduction of rubber plantations in 1876 and the development of tin mining, but the most remarkable impact on a native economy occurred on the Indian subcontinent. Romesh Dutt explains the disastrous consequences of early British rule on the Indian textile industry.

'India in the eighteenth century was a great manufacturing as well as a great agricultural country. It is, unfortunately, true that the East India Company and the British Parliament ... discouraged Indian manufacturers in the early years of British rule in order to encourage the rising manufacturers of England. Their fixed policy ... was to make India subservient to the industries of Great Britain and to make Indian people grow raw produce only, in order to supply material to the looms and manufactures of Great Britain. This policy was pursued ... with total success.'

Thus the Indian textile industry was stifled and millions of artisan workers lost their livelihoods in order to ensure the success of the new textile factories in Lancashire.

The majority of Third World countries have gained independence, but the political and economic interests of developed countries are deeply entrenched in the Third World through the operation of commerce, trade, capital investment and foreign aid programmes. This kind of influence in the countries of the Third World is called **neo-colonialism** because it perpetuates the pattern of dependence established during colonial times and demonstrates the reluctance of developed countries to change the world economic order – to pay higher prices for Third World commodities and to open up their markets to Third World manufactured goods.

---

**Study questions**

1 Explain the connection between colonialism and each of the following: plantations, monoculture, dependent economies, industrial decline.

2 Why are many Third World countries profoundly influenced by developed countries in the post-independence era?

---

*Shortages of capital* The most serious economic bottleneck is the shortage of capital for investment in growth-generating projects. Economic theorists like Rostow attach great importance to the role of capital in economic development and for this reason many developed countries and international banks make substantial loans to help overcome the difficulty of **capital formation** in the Third World. Consequently, some Third World countries have accumulated large debts which further worsen their economic prospects.

The problem of capital deficiency is rooted in the past. In the nineteenth century, it was believed by economists like David Ricardo that the **international division of labour** would result in each country specialising in the production of goods for which it has a **comparative advantage**, and that international trade would lead to **resource equalisation** through the exchange of those goods. But the exchange was far from equal as the developed countries gained a comparative advantage over the Third World – then largely under colonial rule – through the exchange of manufactured goods for commodities as a result of what Raul Prebisch calls the **terms of trade problem**. In effect, the technical benefits of production go only to the developed countries where falling production per unit costs are offset by higher wages and profits for re-investment, research and development. These increased costs, which are built in to the price of manufactured goods, are eventually 'exported' to the Third World as buyers of these goods. The efforts of Third World countries to counteract this problem by industrialisation are frustrated by the imposition of **trade barriers** which restrict the import of foreign manufactured goods into many developed countries. These measures are designed to protect domestic industries but in doing so create an obstacle to economic development in the Third World. A further problem lies in the low and unstable prices of commodities which make up the bulk of Third World exports. In order to obtain fairer and more stable prices a number of Third World countries have joined together into **cartels** or producers unions to control levels of production and prices. The most successful cartel in recent years is OPEC which regulates the price of oil. With the exception of oil, producer-cartels have been unsuccessful in increasing their return on commodities. Indeed, the rising price of oil imposed by the OPEC countries has seriously diminished the relative value of other commodities on which most Third World countries depend (Figure 4.9), thereby further reducing the opportunity to accumulate capital.

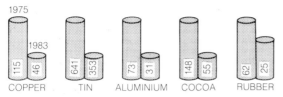

**Figure 4.9** *Number of barrels of oil bought by one tonne of five selected commodities, 1975–83*

In recent years many Third World countries have negotiated foreign loans as a means of obtaining capital for development. The cost of servicing the interest on these loans has led to a serious **debt burden** which has cast a shadow over the economic future of several countries. The newly industrialising countries (NICs) have appeared especially credit-worthy to international institutions like the World Bank as a result of their impressive economic growth in recent years, but some low income countries are getting heavily in debt as developed countries increasingly seek to help the poorest parts of the world (Table 4.3).

In Brazil and many other Third World countries the debt problem escalated after 1973 when oil prices were trebled. Oil imports cost Brazil $605 million or 10% of all imports in 1973 but by 1983, after increasing the volume of imported oil by about a third, the cost had risen to $10 600 million, or nearly half of the value of all imports. To maintain rapid economic growth, the Brazilian Government borrowed heavily from abroad. Now, any growth rate less than 6% per annum represents a **recession** or reduction in national wealth. Brazil, like Nigeria and other indebted countries, has had to reschedule its foreign debts in order to reduce the size of the repayments. Thus, valuable capital is tied up and unavailable for profitable investment in agricultural or industrial projects.

As part of a plan to reduce dependence on imported oil, Brazil has embarked on a search for alternative, cheaper energy sources. It has pioneered the use of sugar-cane for making ethyl alcohol, a substitute for petrol. The National Alcohol Programme was founded in 1975 to promote and finance the new fuel, including a petrol-alcohol mixture called gasohol – 80% petrol and 20% alcohol – for use in ordinary petrol engines, and a 100% alcohol fuel for specially adapted engines in in cars like the Fiat 147. Unlike oil, sugar-cane has the advantage of being a renewable resource and therefore not liable to run out.

**Table 4.3   The debt burden in selected countries**

|  | Growth rate (%) GNP/cap 1960–80 | Interest payments on debts (US$ million) 1970 | 1980 | Debt as a percentage of GNP 1970 | 1980 |
|---|---|---|---|---|---|
| Algeria | 3.2 | 10 | 1305 | 0.9 | 9.5 |
| Brazil | 5.1 | 133 | 4142 | 0.9 | 3.4 |
| Indonesia | 4.0 | 24 | 824 | 0.9 | 2.7 |
| Ivory Coast | 2.5 | 11 | 296 | 2.8 | 8.2 |
| Morocco | 2.5 | 23 | 618 | 1.5 | 6.5 |
| Panama | 3.3 | 7 | 253 | 3.0 | 14.3 |
| Peru | 1.1 | 44 | 547 | 2.1 | 8.1 |
| Senegal | −0.3 | 2 | 57 | 0.8 | 6.9 |
| South Korea | 7.0 | 70 | 1310 | 3.1 | 4.9 |
| Zambia | 0.2 | 23 | 98 | 3.2 | 9.5 |

**Study questions**

1 Briefly explain how international trade increases economic inequality between developed and less developed countries.

2 What is meant by these terms: trade barriers; resource equalisation; cartels; the debt burden?

3 Name two main reasons why international banks are prepared to make loans to Third World countries.

4 Why can it be argued that the debt problem is more serious in low income countries like Zambia than in the middle income countries such as South Korea?

5 Draw histograms to show debt as a percentage of GNP, using the data in Table 4.3. Comment on the pattern of debt for the countries represented.

*Institutional bottlenecks* Much of the impetus for development occurs through major institutions like governments and transnational corporations which are responsible for mobilising resources and promoting economic growth. But in many Third World countries, not only are resources scarce but bottlenecks can prevent their effective use. In extreme cases, the institutions themselves can inhibit development through the misuse or abuse of physical and human resources.

The way in which governments invest national income and overseas loans has a major influence on development. Many Third World governments follow economic growth policies which produce or exaggerate **spatial disparities** in development. The determination of the Brazilian Government to forge an 'economic miracle' in the 1960s led to rapid investment in industry, energy and roads on the market economy model. Most development took place in the relatively prosperous core region of south-east Brazil rather than in the socially and economically deprived regions of the periphery which depended heavily upon agriculture. The low priority given to rural development meant increasing poverty and unemployment in regions like north-east Brazil which are beset by environmental problems and over-dependence on cash crops such as sugar. The unwillingness of many governments to invest in **peripheral regions** and the rural sector is common to many Third World countries where political and economic power is monopolised by a small, wealthy, ruling élite. Such groups often prevent the diffusion of prosperity and scarce resources in order to maintain their position of power and high standard of living often through militarist regimes. Such spatially concentrated patterns of investment are sometimes justified on the grounds that the beneficial effects of prosperity in the core region, including higher employment and productivity in modern industries, will eventually spread to peripheral regions. There is not much evidence to support this theory except in centrally planned countries like China and Cuba where **wealth redistribution** policies have had some success.

Government spending on **non-developmental projects**, like arms, is a serious obstacle to social and economic development. The high priority given to defence is demonstrated in Table 4.4.

Table 4.4 Government expenditure per capita on defence, education and health (US$, 1979)

| | Defence | Education | Health | Defence as a percentage of GNP |
|---|---|---|---|---|
| Egypt | 17 | 24 | 8 | 3.3 |
| Israel | 1083 | 246 | 141 | 29.8 |
| Jordan | 78 | 30 | 13 | 14.2 |
| Mauritania | 35 | 12 | 3 | 14.4 |
| Somalia | 16 | 5 | 2 | 6.8 |
| UK | 249 | 45 | 219 | 5.4 |
| Venezuela | 55 | 101 | 35 | 2.3 |
| Industrial market economies | 283 | 109 | 235 | 3.8 |
| Middle income countries | 39 | 35 | 15 | 3.3 |
| Low income countries | 9 | 4 | 1 | 4.5 |

Military expenditure is dominated by the advanced industrial countries but it consumed a relatively larger proportion of GNP in the Third World (Figure 4.10). One reason for the

Figure 4.10 Military expenditure by major world regions, 1981

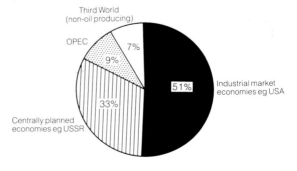

high level of defence spending in the Third World lies in the origins and composition of many governments which have gained power by **military coups** and hold power by force or repression. Sivard claims that two thirds of the military governments in the Third World are classified as highly repressive, that is, they use violence officially and on a large scale.

---

**Study activity**

1 Prepare the arguments for a debate both FOR and AGAINST the build-up of military hardware in the Third World.
2 It is sometimes argued that developed countries like the USA, USSR and Britain 'buy' friends in the Third World with arms deals. See if you can find any evidence for this view.

---

Governments may also impose severe constraints on economic development by inefficiency or pursuing racist policies. Raj Krishna regards bureaucratic overcontrol as the greatest single constraint on industrial growth in India.

'Critical materials are rationed, foreign exchange is rationed, all large investments are licensed after prolonged processing, labour laws are overprotective, taxes are numerous and complex, all key prices are centrally administered, capacity expansion is restricted and there are restrictions on the siting of industries. Corps of civil servants administer their supposedly socialist controls and armies of inspectors collect kickbacks to allow producers to produce.' (adapted from *The Economic Development of India*, R. Krishna in *Scientific American, 1980*).

Where governments follow **racist policies**, the benefits of economic and social progress are made available to only a section of the population. The policy of apartheid, or separate development for black and white people, in South Africa has perpetuated racial and spatial inequalities over the past thirty years. The exploitation of cheap African labour and the setting up of 'bantu homelands' where the families of labourers and non-productive

Africans, such as the elderly and the infirm, live, have contributed to a highly polarised pattern of economic development based on **racial discrimination**. As long as the South African Government implements its apartheid policy it will continue to deny basic social, economic and political rights to the black majority in the country (Figure 4.11).

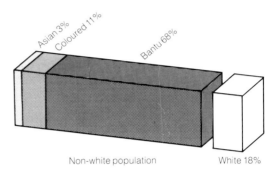

*Figure 4.11    The composition of population in South Africa by race*

In extreme cases, racist policies can actively undermine the development process. The rule of President Amin of Uganda (1971–79) led to the expulsion of the Asian community which played a leading role in the Ugandan economy. There were also mass arrests and the 'disappearance' of nearly half a million people. As a consequence of this catastrophic breach of **human rights** by the Amin Government, Britain terminated its substantial aid programme and the USA imposed a **trade embargo**. The economic and social development of Uganda was set back at least twenty years as a result of this period of misrule. Civil wars caused by political, racial and religious tensions have shattered the economies of several Third World countries, including Vietnam, Kampuchea, the Lebanon, Iran and Iraq. In each case, internal conflict has damaged economic production, disrupted communications and created great human losses and misery. Furthermore, political instability adversely affects external relations with other countries which in turn hinders international co-operation and development.

**Study activity**

Assess the impact of war on the development of one of the following countries: Lebanon; Nicaragua; Angola; Somalia; Vietnam. Refer to newspaper reports and Third World journals such as *South* and the *New Internationalist*.

**Transnational corporations**, sometimes called multinationals, exert a powerful influence on development. Large firms like Shell and IBM which own productive assets such as mines, plantations and factories in more than one country are examples of transnational corporations. About a third of all transnational investment is in the Third World, particularly in resource-rich countries such as

Figure 4.12 *Transnational corporations exert a powerful influence in the Third World in their search for new markets, sources of raw material and locations for factories. Coca Cola is drunk in practically every country in the world*

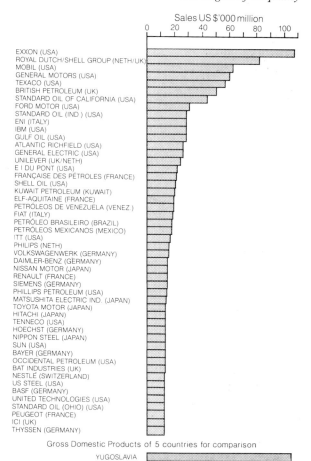

Figure 4.13 *The value of sales by transnational corporations*

Brazil, Mexico and Indonesia where the governments are deemed to be relatively stable and well-disposed towards developed capitalist countries. The sales revenues of transnationals exceed the national incomes of many countries, so it is easy to appreciate the power of these institutions to negotiate deals and expand their economic activities (Figure 4.13). However, transnational operations in the Third World are something of a mixed blessing. The foreign earnings of major mineral companies in particular, such as Rio Tinto Zinc (RTZ) and Royal Dutch Shell, are enormous but they tend to accrue in the parent country rather than in the

49

Third World. Transnational operations generally lead to isolated investment and development in **enclaves** such as mining and lumber camps, industrial enterprise zones and free trade zones provided by the host governments as tax havens for foreign companies (Figure 4.14). The wider benefits of this investment are

*Figure 4.14    The free-trade zone 'carrot'*

lost since the vital **linkage effect** with related industries is missing as the modern enclave development is isolated from the economy of the region in which it is located. Furthermore, transnationals tend to employ foreign technicians and managers and imported technology so the **multiplier effect** which would normally generate associated industries is largely missing. The relatively high incomes of employees often leads to patterns of conspicuous consumption by expatriate and local workers, thus setting up a **social élite** whose standard of living and life style is alien to much of the Third World.

Many Third World Governments are beginning to question the exploitation of their resources by transnationals and to recognise some of the disbenefits they bring. Apart from any economic and social problems, severe environmental damage has followed in the wake

of many transnational operations. If the present rate of exploitation and deforestation continues in the Amazon region of Brazil for example, it is likely to be followed by ecological disaster.

**Study questions**

1 Define a transnational corporation and give some examples.
2 Why do many transnationals invest in the Third World?
3 What are some of the disbenefits that transnational corporations bring to Third World countries?
4 In what ways do the large transnationals have greater power than many individual countries?
5 Why do you think free trade zones are portrayed as a carrot for foreign companies in Figure 4.14.

*The population explosion* The phenomenal growth of population in modern times, sometimes referred to as the 'population explosion', is widely held to be a major obstacle to development, particularly in developing countries where rates of increase are now the highest in the world (Figure 4.15). Nearly two hundred

*Figure 4.15    The growth of world population*

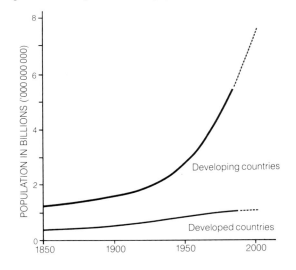

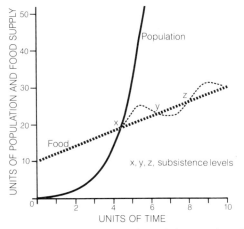

*Figure 4.16  Malthus' predictions of population growth and food supplies*

years ago, Thomas Malthus made gloomy predictions about population growth outstripping food supplies. He argued in his *Essay on the Principle of Population, 1798*, that whereas population increases geometrically (1, 2, 4, 8 etc) the supply of food can only be expanded at an arithmetical rate (1, 2, 3, 4 etc). Following the **Law of Diminishing Returns**, Malthus assumed that land was a fixed factor, so as the population increased the amount of food available per person would gradually decrease until some of the population were forced to live below subsistence level (at $x$, $y$ and $z$ on Figure 4.16). In the absence of **preventive checks** or birth control, Malthus claimed that only **positive checks** like starvation, disease and war would bring the numbers down to a supportable level.

**Study activity**

How far do you think Malthus was correct in saying that land was a fixed factor? Was he right to assume that production would depend solely on the size of population? Using examples of reclamation, drainage, irrigation, and 'the Green Revolution' farming techniques, show how food production has increased in different parts of the world.

Although subsequent events exposed fundamental weaknesses in Malthus' argument, the modern prophets of demographic doom, the **neo-Malthusians** like biologist Paul Erlich, continue to predict mass starvation and **eco-catastrophe** following the destruction of the natural environment by runaway population growth. In their view, those less developed countries that experience recurrent famines are **overpopulated**. They are burdened with excessive numbers of people for the available resources to sustain a reasonable standard of living. The marginal increases or declining wealth per capita occurring in the least developed countries indicates a general decline in levels of living standards for a large proportion of the people in these countries (Figure 4.17).

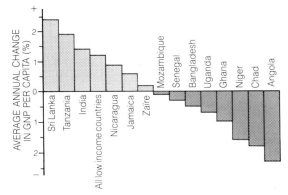

*Figure 4.17  Changes in GNP per capita in selected low income countries, 1960–80*

Malthus' predictions were not realized mainly because he was unable to take account of the massive impact of technological change on agriculture that followed the industrial revolution. As a result of these improvements in farming, the world of the 1980s is characterised by global abundance rather than scarcity (Table 4.5).

Shortages of food and famines tend to be local or regional in scale, resulting from poor distribution of food and poverty. According to John Gribbin some people starve and many more are undernourished because not enough food is available in the right place, at the right time and at the right price.

**Table 4.5   Availability of food**

|  | Percentage of requirements, 1970 | | Index of food production, 1980 (1969–71 = 100) |
|---|---|---|---|
|  | Calories | Protein |  |
| WORLD | 101 | 173 | 106 |
| Developed countries | 121 | 229 | 113 |
| Developing countries | 96 | 147 | 102 |
| Asia | 93 | 141 | 112 |
| Africa | 93 | 141 | 90 |
| Latin America | 106 | 172 | 111 |
| Near East | 97 | 147 | 104 |
| Centrally planned Asia* | 88 | 153 | 117 |

*China, North Korea, Vietnam and Kampuchea.

---

**Study questions**

1 How would population growth be controlled, according to Malthus?

2 Attempt your own definition of the following terms: subsistence level; overpopulation; diminishing returns.

3 Briefly explain the main cause of famines in the Third World today.

4 Describe the availability of food and note the major areas of surplus and shortage (Table 4.5). How might these differences be evened out?

---

In contrast to the Malthusian Model, non-Malthusians view population growth as an essential element in the development process. In developed countries like Britain, rapid economic growth and industrialisation were stimulated by population growth, whether it occurred primarily as a consequence of declining death rates following health and welfare improvements, or through large scale immigration from Europe into North America and Australasia. The expanding population in these regions provided both the workforce to produce goods in the new factories, and the markets to consume the manufactured products. Esther Boserup suggests that population growth also stimulates change in agricultural techniques which allow more food to be produced per unit of land. The **Boserup Model** shows how population pressure induces agricultural change (Table 4.6).

**Table 4.6   The Boserup Model**

| Stage | Cultivation system | Population density |
|---|---|---|
| *Stage 1* | Forest-fallow cultivation: 20–25 years fallow; 1–2 years cultivation | Very sparse |
| *Stage 2* | Bush-fallow cultivation: 6–10 years fallow; 2–8 years cultivation | Sparse |
| *Stage 3* | Short-fallow cultivation: 1–2 years fallow; nearly continuous cultivation | Moderate |
| *Stage 4* | Annual cropping; several months of fallow only; continuous cultivation | Dense |
| *Stage 5* | Multiple cropping: little or no fallow period; several crops grown annually | Very dense |

Further grounds to support a more optimistic view of population lie in the evidence of world demographic trends, and particularly the progress made towards low birth rates in some newly industrialised countries, following the pattern set by the developed countries. This trend, known as the **Demographic Transition**, is generally represented as a sequence of four stages (Figure 4.18). The start of a similar

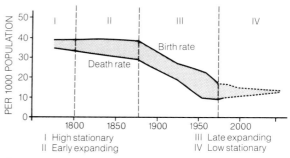

Figure 4.18   The demographic transition in developed countries

sequence can be identified in the pattern of population change in the Third World, although the timing and rate of these changes are significantly different (Figure 4.19). Some Third World countries like South Korea and Singapore have succeeded in reducing the rate

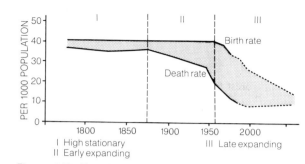

*Figure 4.19 The demographic transition in less developed countries*

**Study activity**

The doubling time of a population can be worked out approximately by dividing the growth rate into 72. Work out the doubling times for the following populations: low income countries (2.1%); middle income countries (2.4%); high income, oil-exporting countries (5.0%); industrial market countries (0.8%); India (1.9%); China (1.2%); Kenya (4.1%); Kuwait (6.0%); United Kingdom (0.2%).

of population growth through rapid economic and social development which now encourages couples to restrict the size of their families. China, too, has made some progress in curbing its massive population by insisting on late marriages and small families. But other countries, like Libya and Chad, are regarded by their governments as underpopulated so they follow **pro-natalist** policies to encourage childbirth, in keeping with Islamic teaching (Table 4.7).

**Table 4.7 Demographic trends in selected countries**

| Country | Birth rate (per 1000 population) 1960 | 1980 | Death rate (per 1000 population) 1960 | 1980 |
|---|---|---|---|---|
| Chad | 45 | 44 | 29 | 24 |
| China | 36 | 18 | 15 | 6 |
| Mexico | 45 | 37 | 12 | 7 |
| Singapore | 38 | 17 | 8 | 5 |
| United Kingdom | 17 | 14 | 12 | 12 |

One way of considering the outlook for the world as a whole is to calculate the time it has taken for the population to double. The world reached its first billion inhabitants around 1800 and two billions by 1925. That is a **doubling time** of 125 years. By 1975, the world's population was 4 billion and it is expected to reach 8 billions in the year 2010.

The high birth rate in many Third World countries results in a large juvenile (under 15) population which imposes a heavy **dependency burden** illustrated by the population pyramids

(Figure 4.20). The juvenile population is usually expressed as a percentage of the total population, typically about 24% in developed countries and over 40% in developing countries where it creates an enormous drain on public expenditure for services such as education and welfare. People are a vital resource for development, but the rapid rate of population increase is not being matched by increased

*Figure 4.20 Population pyramids for a developed and a less developed country*

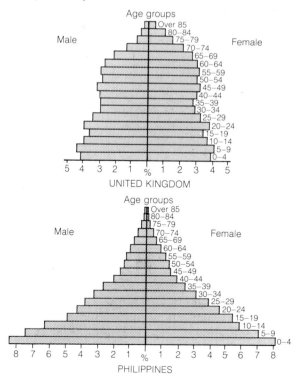

employment and output. For the majority of Third World countries, the population explosion is a serious obstacle to improving the quality of life for a large proportion of the population. In contrast, developed countries like Britain and Japan have an ageing population structure which creates a dependency burden imposed by a high proportion of elderly people.

---

**Study questions**

1 Outline the main differences between Malthusian and non-Malthusian views of population and development.

2 Explain the relationship between high birth rates, ageing populations and the dependency burden.

3 Discuss the significance of the data in Table 4.7 on future population growth in the countries concerned.

4 Comment on the value of the Demographic Transition model for predicting future trends in population growth.

5 What are the main differences between population growth trends and patterns of dependency in developed and developing countries? Refer to Figures 4.18, 4.19 and 4.20.

6 Summarise the main obstacles to economic development discussed in this chapter. Which obstacles, in your view, impose the most severe constraint on development in the Third World?

---

## Theories of development and underdevelopment

There are obstacles to development in every country. Indeed, some of the most highly developed and wealthy countries in the world, like Switzerland and Kuwait, have relatively few advantages for development.

---

**Study activity**

Find out all you can from geography books and encyclopaedias why Switzerland and Kuwait have become wealthy countries. Describe the

---

major obstacles that had to be overcome and the main differences between the development of these two countries. (You can refer to *Recreation and Tourism* in this series for information on one aspect of Switzerland's economic development.)

---

The fact that development can occur in the face of severe obstacles suggests that there are other, more fundamental causes of inequality amongst nations. The search for an explanation of unequal development has led to several theories which draw on both orthodox and radical views of the development process.

**Theories of development** which are based on ideas of modern economic growth may be termed orthodox theories because they reflect the path of economic development followed by the countries of Western Europe and North America. **Theories of underdevelopment** take more account of the widespread and persistent occurrence of poverty, economic stagnation and social deprivation in the less developed countries. These theories provide radical explanations of inequality between countries.

The **vicious circle of poverty theory** attempts to show that poverty is self-perpetuating. 'A country is poor because it is poor' sums up Ragnar Nurkse's view that less developed countries are trapped in a vicious circle of poverty caused by lack of capital and low incomes (Figure 4.21). In fact, this theory explains very little as it cannot account for the emergence of developed countries from their early poverty and subsistence economies. The theory assumes that development takes place in

*Figure 4.21  The vicious circle of poverty*

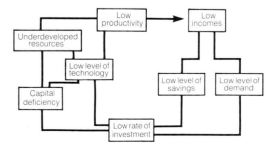

isolation from the rest of the world. Most Third World countries boost their supplies of domestic capital with foreign aid and loans from international banks. There are many signs that less developed countries are developing rapidly. China broke out of centuries of stagnation by revolutionary change inspired by communism. South Korea has become transformed into a modern industrial country by heavy investment in modern technology using large amounts of foreign capital and technical assistance. Most middle income countries and the rich, oil-exporting countries are experiencing so-called economic miracles so it seems that the vicious circle theory can only be applied to the least developed countries with any confidence, but even here, other theories may provide a sounder explanation of underdevelopment.

---

**Study questions**

1 Outline the main difference between theories of development and underdevelopment.
2 What are the weaknesses of the vicious circle of poverty theory?

---

The idea that a country passes from a state of underdevelopment to a state of development through a series of stages of economic growth was advocated by W. Rostow in his popular theory of development. The crucial factor in the **Stages of Economic Growth Theory** is the level of savings necessary to achieve what Rostow called economic 'take-off' (Figure 4.22). He compared development to an aircraft

*Figure 4.22 The Stages of Economic Growth model (after Rostow)*

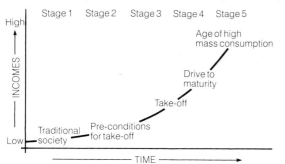

taking off: first it taxies down the runway (a pre-condition for take-off), then it becomes airborne (take-off has occurred) after which it continues to fly (the drive to maturity in Rostow's model). In economic language, national savings should increase from around 5% to 10% or more in order to achieve take-off. But just as an aircraft must continue to use its engines once it has taken off, so a country must continue to develop its economy. It will not happen automatically, as Rostow presumed. So for Rostow, the low level of capital formation is the main cause of poverty and he used this argument to justify the massive transfer of capital from America and the developed countries of the world to the Third World during the 1960s. However, the political motive for these **resource transfers** was very strong, prompted by growing Soviet influence in the newly-independent countries of Africa and Asia. But the removal of one barrier (capital shortage in this instance) does not guarantee development. Rostow's theory fails to take into account several important non-economic factors of development, such as the population explosion, and alternative models of development. Nearly a century earlier, Karl Marx outlined a **political model of development** in which the final stage was communism, when the state runs all the key sectors of the economy. Marx believed that the capitalist model contained the seeds of its own destruction through unrestrained competition, exploitation, social inequality and the class struggle which would end in revolution, as it did in Russia, in 1917. Rostow also intended a political purpose in his model by stating that capitalism was the ultimate goal of development, indicated by a society characterised by high mass consumption of material goods. The main stages of these two theories are compared in Figure 4.23.

The relationship between regions or countries is the key to **core-periphery theories** of development. Friedmann argues that development spreads from developed core regions or countries outwards to backward, peripheral regions. In this model, the world is divided into

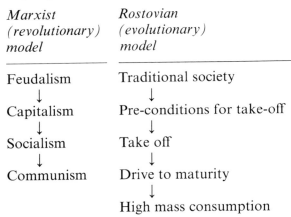

| *Marxist (revolutionary) model* | *Rostovian (evolutionary) model* |
| --- | --- |
| Feudalism | Traditional society |
| ↓ | ↓ |
| Capitalism | Pre-conditions for take-off |
| ↓ | ↓ |
| Socialism | Take off |
| ↓ | ↓ |
| Communism | Drive to maturity |
| | ↓ |
| | High mass consumption |

*Figure 4.23 A comparison of Marx's and Rostow's models of development*

four major regions (Figure 4.24). Eventually, the centre and peripheral regions would merge into a single developed area. This idea is sometimes called **regional convergence**. In a similar theory, Hirschmann believes that development stems from what he called **unbalanced growth**. The stimulus for economic growth would reach less developed countries through the **trickling down process** from the advanced,

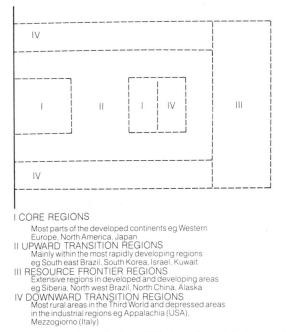

I CORE REGIONS
    Most parts of the developed continents eg Western Europe, North America, Japan
II UPWARD TRANSITION REGIONS
    Mainly within the most rapidly developing regions eg South east Brazil, South Korea, Israel, Kuwait
III RESOURCE FRONTIER REGIONS
    Extensive regions in developed and developing areas eg Siberia, North west Brazil, North China, Alaska
IV DOWNWARD TRANSITION REGIONS
    Most rural areas in the Third World and depressed areas in the industrial regions eg Appalachia (USA), Mezzogiorno (Italy)

*Figure 4.24 A schematic view of Friedmann's model of unequal development*

industrial countries. This process would be offset by the **polarisation effect** whereby some Third World wealth would benefit the core region countries.

The Swedish economist, Gunnar Myrdal, takes a more pessimistic view of the influence of the core region on the periphery, believing that **regional divergence** is more likely to occur (Figure 4.25). In his model, the beneficial or **'spread' effects** of the developed world (core region) on the less developed countries (peripheral region) are outweighed by what he termed the **'backwash' effects** which favour the core region. The joint impact of the backwash effects is to widen the development gap between the core and the periphery. Myrdal described the process as circular and cumulative since the effect of moving labour, capital and goods to the core is likely to bring about a

*Figure 4.25 Spread and backwash effects in Myrdal's model of circular and cumulative causation.*

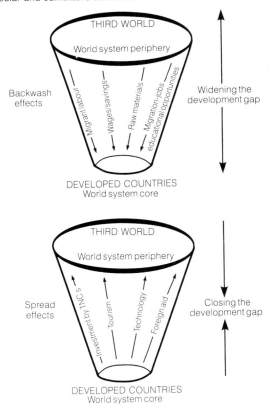

downward spiral of deprivation in the periphery which, in the case of the world system, is the Third World.

Many governments attempt to neutralise backwash effects with policies to help reduce regional inequality. International aid and trade agreements may be seen as ways of reducing inequalities between nations, just as governments implement regional growth strategies within their countries to assist backward or declining regions, as in the case of Brazil's north-east region or the Mezzogiorno of southern Italy.

If orthodox theories of development were correct in their suppositions, then it would be reasonable to expect the abolition of all underdevelopment in the world. Why, then, has this not happened? One answer to this question is provided by writers who advocate radical theories of underdevelopment, like Gundar Frank. Frank asserts that the developed, metropolitan regions such as North America, control and exploit the underdeveloped satellite regions of the Third World. The Frank model shows centre-periphery relationships in terms of **domination and dependence**. For this reason it is referred to as **dependency theory**. According to dependency theory the process of economic development has brought about underdevelopment. The poverty of Third World countries may be attributed to colonial exploitation, political domination and neo-colonialism. Although dependency theory has a strong ideological content in that it is anti-capitalist and anti-imperialist, it nonetheless has value in drawing attention to the fact that developed and underdeveloped regions are part of a single system and therefore connected in some way.

**Study questions**

1 What do you understand by the terms regional convergence and regional divergence?
2 What evidence is there to show that 'spread' effects are outweighed by 'backwash' effects in world development?
3 In what ways does the Marxist model of development differ from Rostow's model?

## Conclusion

There is no simple explanation for the pattern of gross inequality in the world today. To some extent it is the product of historical accident, as a few countries gained an early advantage through industrial expansion and modernisation and were therefore able to develop more rapidly than other parts of the world. It is also due to the presence of obstacles to development which have prevented rapid economic growth in the less developed countries. But the continued persistence of global inequality in the post-colonial period must, in part, be explained by the way in which the world economic system works in favour of the developed countries. Until that system is made more just for Third World countries, it seems unlikely that the symptoms of underdevelopment will be removed.

**Revision**

1 What contribution did the Industrial Revolution make towards the present pattern of global inequality?
2 How far do you think underdevelopment is caused by internal or national factors rather than by external or international factors?

# 5

# Development strategies in the Third World

The widening gap between rich and poor countries, and the massive scale of poverty in the Third World are issues which claim both national and international attention. Many organisations are concerned with solving the problems of underdevelopment, including the governments of developed countries, world bodies like the United Nations and the World Bank and charities like Oxfam. But the most crucial role is played by Third World governments which are responsible for development planning in their own countries.

## Underdevelopment: a suitable case for treatment

The idea of development planning is to look ahead and attempt to bring about improvements in the physical and human environment through the wise use of resources. In a sense it may be compared to a doctor treating a patient. Once the symptoms of the illness have been diagnosed, the doctor prescribes a suitable medicine which should cure the patient. Underdevelopment is, of course, a deep-rooted and persistent 'sickness' which requires more than a single dose of development strategy. Most Third World governments adopt a range of strategies to solve different social and economic problems but since they usually have very limited resources, development planning involves some critical choices. Should priority be given to economic growth by investing in industry or to food production by helping the farmers? Are the problems of malnutrition and illiteracy more urgent than expanding overseas trade? The most wide-spread solutions to underdevelopment involve modernising the traditional economies of developing countries. These solutions generally contain an **urban bias** which favours the ruling classes and wealthy élites, who control the modern economic activities, rather than the mass of the population. But a new perception of underdevelopment is emerging from within the Third World, stressing the problems of human deprivation, rural poverty and economic dependence on rich countries. The solutions to these problems are being sought by some countries through alternative strategies which emphasise rural development and people's basic needs.

Very few Third World countries, notably China, attempt to develop in isolation from the rest of the world. The choice of development strategy is often influenced by economic and political ties with developed countries through trade and aid programmes. These links may restrict the freedom of a less developed country to chose a strategy that is most appropriate to its needs. This aspect of the relationship between developed and less developed countries is illustrated particularly well by the high level of **technological dependence** of the Third World on the countries of Europe, North America and Japan.

> **Study activity**
>
> 1 Discuss the pros and cons of these possible development goals for a Third World country.
>   (a) expand modern manufacturing industry;
>   (b) grow more food;
>   (c) create more jobs;

(d) invest in housing;
(e) improve rural welfare services;
(f) construct nuclear power stations;
(g) buy military equipment from overseas;
(h) extend the national road network;
(i) promote tourism;
(j) build modern hospitals.

**2** Using this list of goals, choose the five you would give priority to in a national development plan. Briefly justify the choice you have made.

**3** In what ways is the analogy between illness and underdevelopment useful or unrealistic?

## The technological choice: men or machines?

The application of science to the production of goods is known as **technology**. Machines are a part of everyday life in developed countries like Britain where even quite young children play games and learn with sophisticated equipment like computers. In most less developed countries, the **level of technological development** is relatively low compared with the advanced technology of developed countries. To a large extent the reason for this **technological gap** lies in the relative availability of two vital **factors of production**, capital and labour. The tools of a village craftsman, for example, are quite cheap to make and operate so they are affordable by people with low incomes. They represent what are called **capital-saving technologies** but they are also labour-intensive since they require manual operation. This type of simple technology is most widespread in rural areas of the Third World where labour is abundant but capital is scarce. There are drawbacks to simple technology. The level of output per worker is very low, so the volume of production is restricted. Furthermore, the range and quality of goods that can be made is limited to everyday goods like utensils, tools and other craft products. In contrast, the advanced technologies of developed countries are relatively expensive and **labour-saving**, like the electronic robots which have largely replaced men in some factory operations, such as car assembly lines.

This kind of technology has high operational costs, (eg the amount of energy used) so it is most widely found in rich, developed countries.

Whatever form it takes, technology plays a crucial role in development. Some economists believe that technology is the key to economic growth and the only way to close the development gap between rich and poor countries is to increase the production of goods in the Third World by introducing more advanced forms of technology. Consequently many Third World governments opt for advanced technology in their development strategies in the belief that it will bring economic growth. They are encouraged to adopt the technologies of developed countries by the relative ease of **technological transfer** from one country to another and the readiness of developed countries and transnational companies to sell them advanced technology. But the adoption of advanced technology can lead to serious problems in developing countries by adding to the level of unemployment and by increasing the burden of debt.

**Study activity**

Assess the possible socioeconomic gains and losses in the following example of technological transfers to the Third World.

The Volta River Project in Ghana was undertaken at a cost of over £100 million. The aim of the project was to build an HEP station at Akosombo and an aluminium smelter at Tema. Bauxite, which could have been mined locally, was imported from Jamaica by the foreign-based company, and the entire production of refined aluminium is exported. The advanced technology of the power station and the smelter has created about a thousand jobs for Ghanaians as well as other fringe benefits, such as free transport. Several villages – 80000 people – had to be moved as Lake Volta filled the valley above the Akosombo Dam. The lake provides fish and some irrigation, and the large supplies of electricity provide power for a textile factory in Akosombo but it has not sparked off widespread industrialisation in Ghana.

**Study questions**

1 Briefly outline your understanding of the terms 'technological dependence' and 'technological transfer'.

2 Describe the nature of the technological gap between developed and less developed countries. Use some of your own examples to illustrate your answer.

3 What are the main disadvantages of (a) advanced technology and (b) simple technology in less developed countries?

*Intermediate technology* What, then, is an appropriate technology for a developing country? E F Schumacher argued that neither capital-intensive nor labour-intensive technologies were ideal for the Third World in his book, *Small is Beautiful*. He introduced the idea of an **intermediate technology** to fill the gap between simple and advanced technologies. It could be achieved in various ways, by up-grading traditional craft technologies like hand-looms, by scaling down high-cost technologies such as modern brick-making methods, and by designing new products and using unconventional sources of power like biogas and the wind. Schumacher defined appropriate technology in terms of the **cost of a workplace**. This figure is calculated by dividing the cost of a factory by the number of jobs it provides. Thus if a factory costs £50000 and provides work for 50 people, then the cost of a workplace will be £1000. A modern brick works costing around £40000 per workplace is far less appropriate to a Third World country than a factory using intermediate technology at a cost per workplace of £400. Furthermore, modern factories often have the capacity to produce far more goods than is required in a developing country and so it would be operated under capacity. Indian steel plants, for example, work at about 60% capacity, which represents a waste of around 40% of capital costs. Intermediate technology allows the volume of supply to be related closely to demand, since it does not rely on mass production technology. Also, by using relatively labour-intensive methods of production, intermediate technology generates employment and helps promote social equality since it does not advantage one group of people with high wages and the special privileges, such as free schooling, that often go with employment in modern industries. For these reasons, intermediate technology has become associated with development strategies that encourage equality, self-reliance and local self-sufficiency.

*Figure 5.1 Spinning silk using 'appropriate' technology in China*

**Study questions**

1 Using the information in Figure 5.1 and Table 5.1, write a short essay on the meaning of appropriate technology.

2 The main characteristics of intermediate technology are summarised below. Use this information to show why it is described as an appropriate technology for the needs of many Third World countries.

Intermediate technology should:

(a) provide new and improved workplaces as near as possible to where people live, that is mainly in rural areas;

(b) be cheap enough to create jobs in large numbers with capital investment in workplaces related to local incomes per person;

(c) use simple methods and place the least possible reliance on imported materials, skills and organisations;

(d) direct production mainly towards meeting local needs using local resources.

**Table 5.1  Three levels of farm technology**

| Level of technology | Example | Cost of buying | Cost of running | Labour saving | Field size | Farm income |
|---|---|---|---|---|---|---|
| Low | Hoe, wooden plough | None | None | Small | Small | Low |
| Intermediate | Pump, hand-operated cultivators | Low | Low | Medium | Medium | Medium |
| Advanced | Tractor, combine-harvester | High | High | Great | Large | High |

## Industrialisation

Some economists think that industrialisation can solve the problems of underdevelopment in the Third World. They point out that countries like the Soviet Union and Japan were relatively backward until large-scale industrialisation took place. The rapid economic development of the newly-industrialised countries of the Third World, notably Brazil, South Korea, Taiwan, Singapore and Hong Kong, testifies to this belief. Even in some very poor developing countries, like India and China, the establishment of modern industries has done much to sustain economic growth in the face of massive population increases over the past 25 years. The arguments in favour of a strategy of industrialisation emphasise the beneficial effects of industry on employment, incomes and trade.

*The multiplier effect* The growth of manufacturing industry leads to employment not

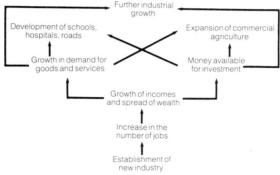

*Figure 5.2  The multiplier effect*

only in factories but also in other economic activities through what is termed the **multiplier effect** (Figure 5.2). The general effect is the expansion of the **modern sector** of the economy, or what Milton Santos calls 'the upper circuit' of the urban economy in less developed countries (Table 5.2). As the incomes of employees in the modern sector are higher than in the traditional sector or lower circuit, so they are

**Table 5.2  The two circuits of the urban economy in less developed countries**

| Characteristic | Upper circuit | Lower circuit |
|---|---|---|
| Technology | Capital intensive | Labour intensive |
| Organisation | Bureaucratic | Primitive |
| Capital | Abundant | Very little |
| Labour | Limited and skilled | Abundant and unskilled |
| Wages | Normal and regular | Rare |
| Prices | Mainly fixed | Negotiable by bargaining |
| Equipment | Extensive and high quality | Small and poor quality |
| Credit | Available from banks | Available from individuals |
| Fixed costs | Substantial | Negligible |
| Advertising | Widespread; essential | None; unnecessary |
| Overhead capital | Essential | Unnecessary |
| Government help | Extensive | None |
| Dependence on foreign countries | Great | None |

able to afford a higher standard of living and better housing. These higher incomes tend to increase the demand for goods which in turn stimulates economic growth.

*Import substitution* As manufacturing industries are set up, the volume and value of imports may be reduced through the process of **import substitution** whereby local factories turn out goods that were previously imported. The main import-substituting industries include processed food and drinks, textiles, clothing and shoes, construction materials like cement and bricks, and in some countries, iron and steel production as a foundation for further industrialisation. By diversifying their predominantly agricultural economies, Third World countries like Mexico and South Korea have reduced their dependence on the production of a few commodities and raw materials for which they receive an uncertain income on the world market due to fluctuating prices.

The process of industrialisation is often accelerated by allowing transnational companies to set up factories and by accepting foreign aid for industrial projects. Some countries, like Sri Lanka and China, have designated enterprise zones where foreign companies reap the benefits of cheap Third World labour and tax concessions. For their part, the host country obtains advanced technology and spin off effects such as training in skills, technical advice and international markets.

*Modernisation* Modern factories in the Third World are symbols of economic progress and modernisation. But it should be remembered that industrialisation rarely involves the mass of population that live in the countryside and, indeed, it can exist side by side with poverty and malnutrition. The spread effects of industrialisation can be directed towards the countryside through an agricultural support policy which encourages the production of farm equipment, fertilizers and other agricultural inputs. Both India and China have adopted this kind of industrial strategy but its success depends upon many factors such as farm size and ownership, credit facilities and the farmer's readiness to adopt new technologies and farming methods.

---

**Study activity**

Find out all you can about the growth of industry in (a) the Soviet Union and (b) Japan. Explain why these are suitable countries to illustrate the effects of industrialisation on development.

**Study questions**

1 What is meant by the 'modern sector of the economy'? Refer particularly to Table 5.2.
2 Why do you think transnational corporations are attracted to Third World countries?
3 How can industrialisation lead to an increase in wealth disparities within a developing country?

---

**Agricultural development**

The reduction of hunger and malnutrition by increasing food supplies is an obvious target for development in the Third World, and yet it is often accorded a fairly low priority in many development plans. As the main purpose of agricultural development is to improve the quantity and quality of farm production, it is particularly appropriate in the Third World where traditional food production systems are relatively inefficient in terms of output per capita compared to many developed countries (Table 5.3). It is also important since most

**Table 5.3 Productivity per head of economically active population in agriculture, 1977 (in US$)**

| Country | Productivity | Country | Productivity |
|---|---|---|---|
| USA | 23 360 | Philippines | 738 |
| UK | 11 071 | Sri Lanka | 512 |
| Argentina | 4 229 | Tanzania | 268 |
| Brazil | 1 123 | India | 189 |
| Mexico | 1 026 | Ethiopia | 118 |

developing countries derive a large proportion of their GNP from agriculture (and some find it necessary to import food from North America and Europe).

The two chief means of increasing agricultural output are by extending the area of cultivated land and by using more intensive methods of farming. Some relatively under-populated countries like Indonesia and Brazil have added to the area of farmland through agricultural settlement schemes in their forest zones. But most agricultural development in the Third World consists of efforts to intensify the use of existing farmland through the application of scientific methods of cultivation. The main areas of progress include plant research, irrigation, and modern farm technology.

*The Green Revolution* In the early 1960s crop research scientists in Mexico and the Philippines achieved a breakthrough by producing high-yielding varieties (HYVs) of wheat and rice. The dramatic increase in crop yields that followed this research was heralded as the **Green Revolution.** The new, improved seeds made a significant impact on agricultural yields, doubling and trebling the size of annual harvests in parts of South East Asia (Figure 5.3). The success of the Green Revolution has been patchy as it depends upon farmers using the correct **agricultural inputs** to ensure improved yields (Table 5.4).

From this table it can be seen that the new

**Table 5.4   The cost of 'ordinary' and 'miracle' rice farming in the Philippines**

| Items | Costs (in Philippine pesos) Miracle rice | Ordinary rice |
|---|---|---|
| 1   Preparing the land | 98 | 85 |
| 2   Transplanting | 62 | 52 |
| 3   Care of crops | 71 | 32 |
| 4   Harvesting | 218 | 152 |
| 5   Drying and hauling | 44 | 13 |
| Total labour costs | 493 | 334 |
| 6   Seeds | 24 | 24 |
| 7   Fertilizers | 189 | 47 |
| 8   Insecticides | 85 | 6 |
| 9   Irrigation | 30 | 30 |
| Total cost of materials | 328 | 107 |
| Grand total cost | 821 | 441 |
| Rice yield per hectare* | 4.5 | 1.5 |
| Income per hectare | 1659 | 391 |

*in tonnes.

'miracle' seeds require the right amount of fertilizers, insecticides and irrigation to give high yields. Without insecticides, crop losses can amount to 40% of the total harvest. The new agricultural package of technology necessary for Green Revolution farming requires, therefore, some technical knowledge, so **farm extension services**, which help educate farmers, play an important role in agricultural development. The State of Punjab in India is one of the most successful Green Revolution farming areas. In 1972, after six years of planting HYVs, yields of both rice and wheat had risen sharply and farm incomes had doubled (Figure 5.4). The Green Revolution has made a substantial contribution to foodgrain production in India though it has also made food more expensive. Consequently, **food security** – access to regular, adequate nourishment – remains a serious problem, especially amongst the urban poor who cannot afford to buy food at market prices. While the success of the Green Revolution was ensured by the extensive irrigation network in the Punjab, many farmers in the Third World rely on **rain-**

*Figure 5.3* Agricultural development in Indonesia. Fertilizer is being applied to a high-yielding variety of rice

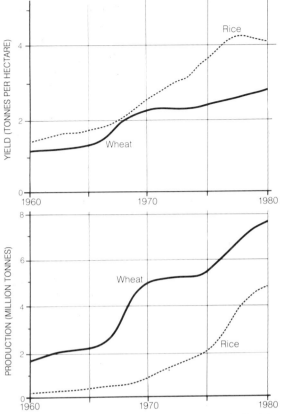

*Figure 5.4* The effects of the Green Revolution in the Punjab of India

**fed cultivation**. The Puebla Project in Mexico has succeeded in developing new maize varieties which give three to four times the normal yield in unirrigated areas. As irrigation is very expensive to develop, the Mexican programme of rain-fed agriculture may be appropriate to farming in other regions with similar climatic conditions, where irrigation is not available, such as parts of West and East Africa.

*Mechanisation* The labour-intensive methods of farming in the Third World are a serious drawback to agricultural development. The increased use of machinery has made an impressive contribution to productivity in regions like the Punjab where the process of **tractorisation** is well advanced. However, the high cost of tractors, the small size of fields and fragmented land ownership render farm mechanisation

quite impractical in many parts of the Third World. The Chinese have overcome some of these problems by developing small motorised cultivators – 'walking' tractors – and intermediate technology solutions, such as rice-planting machines. A further problem arises from the effect of mechanisation on rural employment. It releases farm workers from the toil associated with ploughing, sowing and harvesting, but in countries like India which have high levels of **rural underemployment**, mechanisation is a mixed blessing.

Table 5.5  **World foodgrain consumption in kg/capita**

|  | 1961–64 | 1970–73 | 1976–79 |
|---|---|---|---|
| World total | 312.1 | 342.8 | 362.1 |
| All low income countries | 207.1 | 202.7 | 202.4 |
| Sub-Saharan Africa | 159.5 | 151.9 | 141.3 |
| All middle income countries | 238.1 | 255.6 | 275.7 |
| Latin America | 235.7 | 244.0 | 249.1 |

**Study activity**

1 It is generally accepted that the consumption of grain is related both to production and to wealth. Thus it should follow that the world's poorest countries consume the least amount of grain. The activities below are based on Table 5.5 which shows grain consumption data between 1961–64, and 1976–79.

(a) Calculate the percentage change in foodgrain consumption for each region between 1961–64 and 1976–79.

(b) Comment on the trends in world foodgrain consumption indicated by the data in the table and in your calculation.

(c) Why are the figures both optimistic and pessimistic about world grain supplies?

(d) How far do you agree with the opening statement in this study activity?

2 There is now a worldwide network of internationally-funded agricultural research centres whose aim is to improve crop and livestock production throughout the Third World. Each centre specialises in a particular type of agriculture.

- The International Rice Research Institute (IRRI), at Los Banos in the Philippines, where the 'miracle' rice seeds were developed under the sponsorship of the Rockefeller and Ford Foundations in the 1960s.
- The International Maize and Wheat Improvement Centre (CIMMYT), set up in 1966 at El Batan in Mexico, developed wheat and maize varieties suited to semi-arid conditions.
- The International Centre of Tropical Agriculture (CIAT), at Palmira, in Colombia, applies its expertise to the development of effective farming systems in lowland tropical regions.
- The International Institute for Tropical Agriculture (IITA), Ibadan, Nigeria, specialises in tropical farming in the humid tropical regions, mostly in Africa.
- The International Potato Centre (CIP), Lima, Peru, researches into improved potato production mainly for countries in Latin America.
- The International Crops Research Institute for the Semi-Arid Tropics (ICRISAT), Hyderabad, India, stresses farming systems and water conservation methods.
- The International Laboratory for Research on Animal Diseases (ILRAD), Nairobi, Kenya, is currently concentrating on immunological methods for controlling animal diseases (eg East Coast Fever and trypanosomiasis).

(a) Find out what you can about these research centres and the contribution they make towards agricultural development in the Third World.

(b) Try to arrange a visit to a local agricultural research centre and look at the work being carried out there.

## Rural development

It is estimated that about 800 million people – a fifth of mankind – are unable to secure the basic necessities of life. These people live in **absolute poverty**, concerned solely with day to day survival. The majority of these people are found in the rural areas of the Third World; and in the least developed countries like Ban-gladesh, one person in three suffers from **rural deprivation** which means inadequate incomes, food and housing. The aim of rural development strategies is to materially improve the lot of the rural poor. This approach to development has gained increasing support from international agencies, such as the International Fund for Agricultural Development which was set up in 1977 to help raise food production and consumption amongst the poor, and from aid organizations concerned with funding Third World projects. The most serious rural problems concern the distribution and ownership of land, and the poorly developed **rural infrastructure**, that is, the provision of welfare services, roads, water and electricity.

*Land reform* Most peasant farms in the Third World are scattered on small plots, usually as a result of the widespread tradition of **inheritance**. Under this system, land is inherited by the surviving sons in a family and so farms become subdivided into increasingly small, fragmented plots with each generation. The pattern of **fragmentation** leads to inefficient farming methods and impedes developments such as irrigation and mechanisation which require large fields to be most effective. A significant proportion of farmland in developing countries is in the hands of a relative small number of landowners, especially in Latin America. Most peasant farmers are either **tenants**, paying high rents to landlords, or **sharecroppers**, giving a proportion of their harvest to the owner. In both cases, the farmer has little incentive to improve the farm and increase crop yields as the benefits would go to the landowners. To combat this problem, **land reform** is urgently needed to **consolidate** uneconomic plots of land into larger, more viable units, and to redistribute land more fairly amongst the farmers. But land reform is a long-term solution which some governments are unwilling to encourage for political reasons. There has been some land reform in Mexico and Bolivia but productivity tended to suffer as rich landowners took their capital away from the farms. **Decapitalisation** is a problem where large estates are broken up. In India, the process of land reform is frustrated by lack of enforcement and **conservatism** amongst peasant farmers. As an alternative to the redistribution of land amongst private owners, some socialist countries, notably China and Cuba, have established **state farms** owned by the government, and **co-operatives** which are run communally by farmers on behalf of the state. This type of land reform generally follows revolutionary struggles in which the interests of the peasant population are uppermost. In Tanzania, agriculture was **socialised** after independence as part of government policy to achieve self-reliance.

*Agrarian reform* Rural development strategies also involve a wide range of **agrarian reforms** which are designed to improve living standards in the countryside. Amongst the main reforms are the provision of cheap credit for farmers,

the initiation of co-operatives to help farmers buy and sell goods, the building of schools and health centres, the improvement of roads and the provision of clean water and electricity.

---

**Study questions**

1 Using Figure 5.5, describe the main problems of rural development in the Third World.
2 Briefly explain the difference between land reform and agrarian reform.
3 Why do you think Third World governments should give priority to rural development strategies?

---

## Welfare development

The growing realisation that mass poverty and social deprivation in the Third World have not been reduced by world economic expansion during the last three decades has contributed towards a re-assessment of the goals of devel-

*Figure 5.5  A typology of rural problems in the Third World*

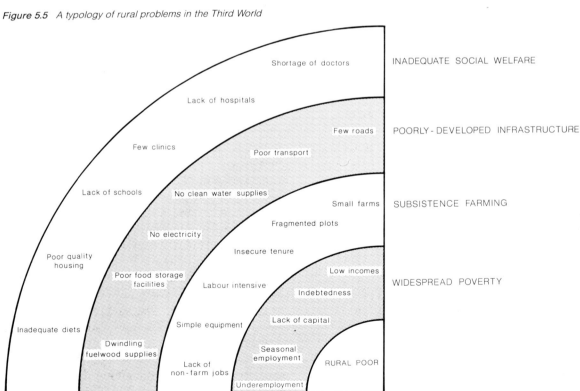

opment. Some less developed countries, like Tanzania and China, have seen an urgent need to adopt alternative development strategies to the prevailing western model of economic growth. This new strategy is oriented towards seeking Third World rather than developed world solutions to their problems.

*Basic needs and self-reliance* The alternative strategy contains three basic objectives. First, development should be directed towards the **eradication of poverty** and the **satisfaction of basic needs.** Everybody should have a basic minimum standard of living with adequate supplies of food and clean water, proper shelter, good health and education. Second, Third World countries should become more **self-reliant,** using local skills and resources rather than relying on foreign expertise and influence. The amount of foreign control in agriculture, mining, forestry and manufacturing industry and the flow of resources abroad should be reduced, giving greater independence from foreign countries. Third, development should be in harmony with the environment to ensure that ecosystems are not irrevocably damaged by exploitation. This approach should also help to prevent the rapid depletion of natural resources for short-term economic gains by establishing long-term **conservation policies.**

The welfare approach to development provides a realistic way of solving the problems of poverty and social deprivation in the Third World. By advocating self-help and low-cost methods of production using intermediate technology, it encourages relatively poor communities to improve their standard of living without drastically altering traditional methods of subsistence agriculture and social values. Unlike strategies to industrialise and modernise Third World countries, this approach to development contains a **rural bias** in its emphasis on people and communities in the countryside. Significant, too, is the effect of this strategy on stemming the tide of **rural–urban migration** as improved living conditions will reduce the rural **'push effects'** that make people

look for a better life in the cities. This is certainly the case in China where the government, in addition to raising living standards in the countryside, has actively discouraged migration to the cities. The basic needs approach to development is particularly appropriate for the world's least developed countries where eating properly and having a decent shelter to live in are luxuries for many people.

---

**Study questions**

1 Why is the basic needs approach to development sometimes referred to as an 'alternative development strategy'?

2 Explain why the basic needs and self-reliance strategy is particularly appropriate for the world's least developed countries.

---

## International trade

For most countries, international trade is the engine of economic growth. They export goods in order to accumulate wealth and pay for imports. But the economic development of many Third World countries is hindered by their dependence on a narrow range of primary projects, restricted overseas markets and declining **terms of trade** which means the value of their exports is declining in relation to the cost of imports. The present pattern of international trade – the exchange of goods between countries – works in favour of the industrial nations of the North rather than equally between all countries. Since the 1960s, the value of commodities like coffee and tea, and the raw materials on which the Third World depends has declined relative to the cost of manufactured goods which are mainly produced in the industrial countries. A notable exception to this general rule is the price of oil which went up rapidly in the 1970s, as the oil-producing countries of the Middle East were in a strong bargaining position. According to classical economic theory, each country should specialise in production for which it has a comparative advantage, such as mining in Zambia, agriculture in New Zealand and industry in Britain. Through the process of **free trade** these products would be exchanged for the mutual benefit of all producing countries. In reality, international trade was established in the eighteenth century between European powers and their colonies in an unequal partnership. The colonies became markets for industrial goods in exchange for cheap raw materials. The colonial pattern of trade has persisted as commodity prices continue to rise more slowly and fluctuate more severely than the price of manufactured goods (Figure 5.6).

**Table 5.6  Percentage share of world exports by major region, 1955–80**

| Region | 1955 | 1980 |
|---|---|---|
| All developing countries | 27.3 | 21.4 |
| Low income countries | 5.6 | 1.9 |
| Middle income countries | 21.7 | 19.5 |
| High income oil-exporting countries | 2.1 | 10.2 |
| All developed countries | 70.6 | 68.4 |
| Europe | 36.1 | 38.5 |
| USA | 16.5 | 10.9 |
| Japan | 2.1 | 6.5 |
| World | 100.0 | 100.0 |

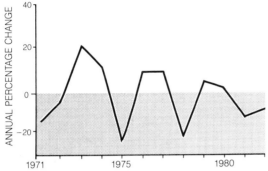

*Figure 5.6* Fluctuations in the price of Third World commodities based on a sample of 33 commodities excluding oil

**Study questions**

1 How does international trade work against the good of Third World countries?
2 Why were the oil-producing countries able to secure high prices for their oil exports?

The Third World's share of international trade has always been quite small. Although the volume of exports has risen substantially over the past thirty years, the share of the world total has dropped to less than a quarter (Table 5.6). This situation disguises the uneven share of output from countries within the Third World. Newly industrialising countries like Brazil and South Korea have expanded their exports very much more than low income countries which still have very undiversified economies and a limited range of goods for export.

*Trading agreements* Third World governments argue that the existing pattern of international trade is a major obstacle to development. However, the issue of commodity prices can only be resolved by international agreements. In 1948 the General Agreement on Tariffs and Trade – GATT – was set up to try and lay down rules for fair trade. But **protectionist policies** followed by many developed countries in Europe and North America to protect their own industries from competition by cheap imports, prevented any significant progress. The United Nations Conference on Trade and Development – UNCTAD – attempted to improve North–South trading relationships by introducing what it called a Generalised System of Preferences for trade with developing countries. While some agreements were reached, UNCTAD failed to get radical changes such as the removal of all **trade barriers** between countries. Many developed countries continued to impose **tariffs** or customs duties on imports like textiles, clothing and electronics equipment.

**Study activity**

1 Draw two divided circle diagrams to illustrate the data in Table 5.6. Comment on the way in which the pattern of world exports has changed since 1955.

2 The EEC's Common Agricultural Policy (CAP) is aimed at achieving self-sufficiency in basic foodstuffs within the Community, thereby excluding, as far as possible, farm produce from outside, including the Third World. Find out all you can about the CAP and how it affects trade between the Community and Third World countries.

The way to increase Third World participation in world trade lies in international efforts to stabilise the price of commodities and to remove tariff barriers on processed goods from the Third World like textiles, sugar and refined metals such as copper. These were among the main recommendations concerning the restructuring of global economic relationships made by the Brandt Commission in 1980. There are also opportunities to increase the volume of trade between Third World countries, and for the formation of economic blocs like the EEC which have greater bargaining power than individual countries.

### Resource transfers and foreign aid

Most developing countries can draw on resources from overseas to help finance development projects. The Victoria Dam project in Sri Lanka illustrates the value of **resource transfers**. It consists of a major dam, reservoir, tunnels and HEP station, which will increase the country's electrical generating capacity by 50% and make it possible to irrigate land for over one million families, thus ending centuries of drought-prone agriculture. The power will feed the national grid and supply foreign-owned manufacturing industries in Colombo's recently-established Free Trade Zone. It will release Sri Lanka from dependence on imported oil which, it is calculated, will cost two and a half times more than locally produced HEP. The project was financed with foreign aid, including £110 million from Britain which was the major donor country.

*Resource transfers* are available as foreign aid, loans from development banks, like the World Bank, and private foreign investment through commercial companies such as transnational corporations. Most loans and foreign investments are made at commercial rates of interest which can lead to debt burdens and substantial repayments. Foreign aid, on the other hand, is usually made at lower or concessional rates of interest which often include a non-repayable **grant element**. The basic purpose of such resource transfers is to help solve the problem of **capital-deficiency**, which is a major obstacle to development in the Third World, and to help developing countries move away from labour-intensive, subsistence and primary producing economies (Figure 5.7).

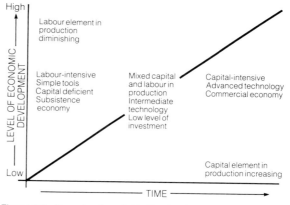

*Figure 5.7   The role of capital in the development process*

*Foreign aid* refers to any form of **official development assistance** which is defined as loans and grants for development purposes made between governments at concessional rates. Most aid is between a donor and recipient country, and therefore called **bilateral aid**, as in the case of British aid to Sri Lanka. When aid is provided by a group of countries such as the EEC or OPEC, it is known as **multilateral aid**. In 1983, 60% of British aid was given bilaterally, with the remaining 40% being chanelled through multilateral agencies such as the EEC, the World Bank and United Nations agencies for development (Figure 5.8).

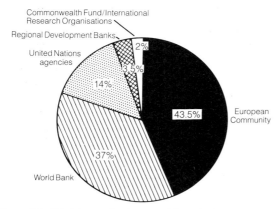

Figure 5.8 *Britain's contribution to multilateral aid agencies, 1982*

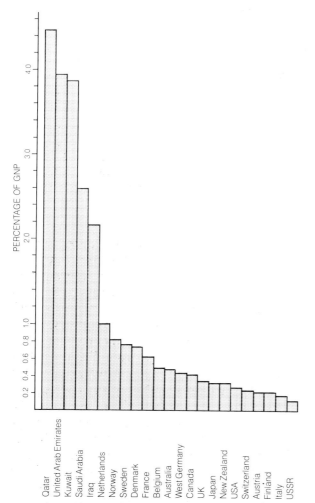

Figure 5.9 *Official development assistance from the developed countries*

The amount of foreign aid provided by developed and oil-rich countries varies, but few donor countries have met the target set by the United Nations of 0.7% of GNP (Figure 5.9). The principal aid donors are the nineteen member countries of the OECD – the Organization for Economic Co-operation and Development – representing the industrial countries of the North, the countries belonging to OPEC and the Soviet Union (Table 5.7). In recent

Table 5.7   **Major sources of aid, 1983**

| Source | Percentage of all aid | Total value of aid ($bn) | Percentage of GNP |
|---|---|---|---|
| OECD countries | 68.6 | 25.9 | 0.35 |
| OPEC countries | 20.6 | 7.8 | 1.46 |
| Communist countries | 5.5 | 2.1 | 0.14 |
| Non-government agencies | 5.3 | 2.0 | 0.02 |

years, some aid has been provided by less developed countries, and China, in particular, has given aid for agriculture and communications in parts of Africa. The volume of aid in relation to all resource transfers remains quite small. In spite of recent efforts to direct aid to the poorest countries, the flow of aid per capita is still higher to middle income countries. There is strong political motivation for the flow of much foreign aid. Israel is an outstanding example (Table 5.8). The value of aid given to Third World countries represents about 8% of their total export earnings so it is easy to understand why many of their governments call for more trade and less aid.

**Study questions**

1 Describe three main forms of resource transfer to the Third World.
2 What is the particular value of foreign aid as opposed to other forms of resource transfer?
3 How far has the United Nations aid target been achieved?
4 Why do you think trade is more important to developing countries than aid?

**Table 5.8  Fifty leading recipients of aid from OECD countries in 1982**

| Recipient countries | Total aid ($ million) | Aid per capita ($) | GNP per capita ($) | Recipient countries | Total aid ($ million) | Aid per capita ($) | GNP per capita ($) |
|---|---|---|---|---|---|---|---|
| 1  Egypt | 1529 | 38.4 | 580 | 26  Burkina Faso | 189 | 33.1 | 190 |
| 2  India | 1419 | 2.1 | 240 | 27  Jamaica | 171 | 77.7 | 1030 |
| 3  Turkey | 850 | 18.7 | 1460 | 28  Niger | 169 | 31.9 | 330 |
| 4  Bangladesh | 838 | 9.3 | 120 | 29  Mali | 167 | 24.2 | 128 |
| 5  Indonesia | 838 | 5.7 | 420 | 30  Malaysia | 166 | 12.3 | 1670 |
| 6  Israel | 826 | 211.8 | 4500 | 31  Tunisia | 162 | 25.3 | 1310 |
| 7  Pakistan | 477 | 5.8 | 300 | 32  Mexico | 162 | 2.4 | 2130 |
| 8  Tanzania | 453 | 25.0 | 280 | 33  Ivory Coast | 156 | 18.1 | 1150 |
| 9  Sri Lanka | 446 | 30.1 | 270 | 34  Algeria | 155 | 8.2 | 1920 |
| 10  Philippines | 412 | 8.6 | 690 | 35  Mozambique | 154 | 14.7 | 270 |
| 11  China | 403 | 0.4 | 290 | 36  Cameroon | 146 | 17.4 | 670 |
| 12  Thailand | 396 | 8.5 | 670 | 37  Nigeria | 132 | 1.6 | 1010 |
| 13  South Korea | 388 | 10.0 | 1520 | 38  Madagascar | 121 | 14.0 | 350 |
| 14  Sudan | 348 | 18.9 | 470 | 39  Nepal | 115 | 8.0 | 140 |
| 15  Brazil | 332 | 2.8 | 2050 | 40  Rwanda | 113 | 22.1 | 200 |
| 16  Morocco | 325 | 16.0 | 860 | 41  Surinam | 112 | 320.0 | 2840 |
| 17  Burma | 317 | 9.5 | 180 | 42  El Salvador | 108 | 24.0 | 590 |
| 18  Papua New Guinea | 303 | 101.0 | 780 | 43  Burundi | 93 | 22.6 | 200 |
| 19  Zaire | 273 | 9.6 | 220 | 44  Vietnam | 92 | 1.7 | 190 |
| 20  Kenya | 260 | 16.3 | 420 | 45  Ethiopia | 92 | 2.9 | 140 |
| 21  Senegal | 244 | 42.8 | 450 | 46  Malawi | 91 | 15.4 | 230 |
| 22  Somalia | 234 | 60.0 | 380 | 47  Uganda | 90 | 6.8 | 280 |
| 23  Zambia | 218 | 37.6 | 560 | 48  Ghana | 90 | 7.7 | 420 |
| 24  Zimbabwe | 217 | 29.3 | 630 | 49  Portugal | 86 | 8.7 | 2370 |
| 25  Peru | 200 | 11.4 | 930 | 50  Haiti | 83 | 16.6 | 270 |

Source: *OECD Development Co-operation 1982 Review.*

Most developing countries receive aid, but international policies now state that aid should be concentrated in the least developed countries. In regions hit by natural disasters such as the Sahel in Africa **emergency aid** is available through organizations like UNDRO – the United Nations Disaster Relief Organization. Some aid strategies, like the EEC's Food Aid for Development Programme, focus on particular economic or social problems. But the provision of **food aid** should be a short-term strategy, integrated with agricultural development plans in order to prevent permanent dependence on free food supplies which would be a major disincentive to growing food locally. The most valuable kind of help is long-term **structural aid** which helps built up agriculture, manufacturing, transport and services like education. With this kind of aid, developing countries can lay the foundation for **self-sustained growth** and eventual independence from aid programmes.

Many aid programmes are to some extent motivated by economic and political self-interest on the part of the donor country. In the Victoria Dam project, Sri Lanka contracted to buy goods and services from Britain. Most developed countries have aid-financed orders which help subsidise industry and create jobs. The political motive for aid often takes the form of supplying and servicing military equipment, as in Israel, or, in the case of the Soviet Union in Afghanistan, giving direct military assistance. But **tied aid** is less useful to Third World countries than **untied aid** because it prevents them from 'shopping around' and getting the best deal.

## Conclusion

The problems of underdevelopment in the Third World are brought about by a combination of internal and external obstacles to development. The idea of development strategies is to overcome, at least partially, some of these obstacles. The governments of developing countries can do much to solve their own problems by investing in projects which generate economic growth and social well-being. But they are also locked into the world economic system through international trade, resource transfer agreements, and political ties over which they have little control so they cannot always develop independently. Increasingly, discussions between the developed and less developed countries, sometimes referred to as the **North–South dialogue**, are seeking ways of improving the world economic system to make it fairer for the countries of the South. In the foreseeable future, the most serious problems of underdevelopment, for which there are no easy solutions, will continue to occur in the least developed countries as the gap between them and other Third World countries widens.

**Revision**

1 Discuss the pros and cons of different forms of technology that may be adopted in a strategy of agricultural and industrial development in the Third World.

2 Review the relative benefits of trade and aid in Third World economic development.

3 What do you consider should be the main topics for discussion in the North–South dialogue?

*Figure 5.10* Who gets aid in the Third World? *(from* South, *March 1984)*

# 6

# Five case studies of development in the Third World

The case studies described in this chapter represent five contrasting approaches to development in the Third World. They include a broad range of strategies designed to alleviate the effects of underdevelopment in both low and middle income countries. In each case study, the main obstacles to development are outlined before the plans and policies that have been adopted to promote development are considered.

## Tanzania

Tanzania is one of the world's poorest and least developed countries. In 1981, the World Bank placed it 102nd out of 125 countries in terms of GNP per capita. The development of Tanzania has been inhibited by a lack of natural resources, a tropical climate subjected to marked seasonal variations in rainfall and prolonged droughts, and a small, predominantly scattered farming population. In addition to this unpromising resource base, the Tanzanian government under President Nyerere inherited a poorly developed colonial economy when Tanzania came into being as an independent country in 1964. Some important aspects of Tanzanian economic development are shown in Figure 6.1.

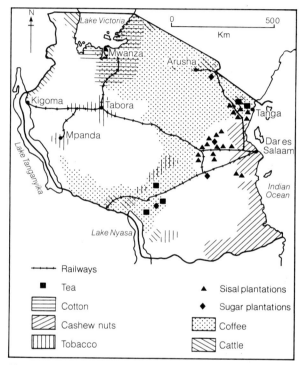

Figure 6.1  Tanzania

*Rural development and ujamaa* Tanzania has followed a radical development strategy aimed at achieving a self-reliant, socialist society. The cornerstone of this policy lies in the programme of rural development and co-operative production known as **ujamaa**. This strategy gained momentum after the Arusha Declaration in 1967 when Nyerere outlined his plans for introducing ujamaa villages. The idea was to move Tanzania's predominantly dispersed rural population into co-operative villages in a

**Figure 6.2** *This co-operative building scheme in Mwamashele is typical of many ujamaa villages in Tanzania*

process of **villagisation** (Figure 6.2). Each village was located close to a road and was planned to house between 250 and 1500 people. In exchange for their co-operation, the peasant families would get a permanent water supply, famine relief, schools and health services. The long-term objective of ujamaa was to raise living standards in the countryside and increase agricultural production in order to achieve self-reliance in basic foodstuffs. The World Bank approved a package of seeds and fertilizers to assist in agricultural development. But according to many reports from ujamaa villages, the policy of villagisation has failed to meet most of its objectives. Many Tanzanian farmers have resented the compulsory eviction from their land and often found the sites of the new villages unprepared and in areas of poor soil fertility. Initially, much productive labour went into clearing land for houses and fields with the result that little food was grown. Perhaps the most serious weakness in the whole enterprise lay in the origins of villagisation, as the brainchild of bureaucrats living in the capital, Dar-es-Salaam, far away from the realities of rural Tanzania, and not as a grass roots movement.

### Study questions

Read the following extracts about rural development in Tanzania.

'If we want to develop, we have no choice but to bring both our way of living and our way of farming up to date. The hand-hoe will not bring us the things we need today. We have got to begin using the plough and the tractor instead. But our people do not have enough money and nor has the government, to provide each family with a tractor. So what we must do is to try and make it possible for groups of farmers to get together and share the cost and the use of a tractor between them. But we cannot even do this if our people are going to continue living over a wide area, far apart from each other. The first and absolutely essential thing to do, therefore, if we want to be able to start using tractors for cultivation, is to begin living in proper villages.' (Nyerere, 1967)

'In many villages physical coercion was used, resulting in hardships to the peasants and some destruction of property. ... No elaborate preparations were taken in moving the peasants at Bigwa. Army lorries were used in moving the peasants, who were caught by surprise, although they were aware that the government had decided to implement the villagisation programme as was happening elsewhere in the region. The peasants were bundled into the lorries and dumped at Misongeni, for most of them hardly a mile from their homes. The place was overgrown with thorny bushes and the quality of land was unquestionably below that of Bigwa....' (Lwoga, 1978)

1 What arguments does President Nyerere put forward in favour of ujamaa villages?

2 Why was the villagisation policy generally unpopular with many peasant farmers and particularly the wealthier ones?

3 The percentage of Tanzania's population living in ujamaa villages is shown for each region in Figure 6.3.

(a) Draw a choropleth (shading technique) map to show the general pattern of villagisation in Tanzania. Use no more than 5 categories, eg under 65; 66–75; 76–85; 86–95; over 95.

(b) Describe the distribution of villagisation shown on your map.

(c) Why do you think the pattern of villagisation is uneven? Your answer should refer to information in Figure 6.1.

4 Why do you think food production in Tanzania decreased in the late 1960's and early 1970's as a result of villagisation?

*Figure 6.3* Percentage of Tanzanian population living in ujamaa villages

| Ar | Arusha | Mo | Morogoro |
|----|--------|----|----------|
| Co | Coast | Mt | Mtwara |
| Do | Dodoma | Mw | Mwanza |
| Ir | Iringa | Rk | Rukwa |
| Is | Isles | Ru | Ruvuma |
| Kg | Kigoma | Sh | Shinyanga |
| Ki | Kilimanjaro | Si | Singida |
| Li | Lindi | Tb | Tabora |
| Ma | Mara | Ta | Tanga |
| Mb | Mbeya | We | West Lake |

**Table 6.1  The growth of Tanzania's parastatal assets (millions of shillings)**

| Sector | Value of assets in 1964 | Value of assets in 1971 |
|--------|-------------------------|-------------------------|
| Manufacturing | 25 | 1 109 |
| Mining | 241 | 311 |
| Construction | 25 | 162 |
| Electricity | 231 | 525 |
| Transport | — | 368 |
| Tourism | 15 | 157 |
| Commerce | 13 | 514 |
| Agriculture | 56 | 250 |
| Finance | 4 | 183 |
| TOTAL | 610 | 3 579 |

*Industrial policy* Tanzania's development strategy of self-reliance has been furthered by the introduction of government corporations known as **parastatals** to run major companies, banks, industries, power suppliers and transport. Their purpose was to limit the transfer of profits out of the country, to invest in productive economic activities like agriculture, manufacturing and tourism and to improve the basic infrastructure by developing energy supplies and transport. The extent to which some of these objectives were realized can be seen in Table 6.1.

Tanzania's programme of industrialisation was set out in the first two Five Year Plans (1964–69; 1969–74), but it was seriously undermined by shortages of capital so progress has been very slow. The manufacture of goods like cement, drink, cigarettes and shoes rose considerably in an effort to reduce the cost of imports. But expenditure on machines and transport equipment rose more rapidly with the effect of pushing up Tanzania's import bill.

Some of the problems of industrialisation are illustrated by the Tanga fertilizer factory, the country's most expensive investment in modern industry. The plant was built using West German credit and it uses imported raw materials to make chemical fertilizers. After it opened, the factory ran at 50% capacity due to operational difficulties. Using high-cost energy and making a product that few farmers could afford, the project had dubious value in the Tanzanian economy.

*Trade and aid* Between 1964 and 1967, the price of sisal, Tanzania's chief export crop, fell from £100 a ton to £60 a ton. With falling export earnings, Tanzania turned increasingly to foreign aid to finance development projects, but borrowing left the country with expensive repayments and a balance of payments problem as the cost of imports overtook the value of exports (Table 6.2). The Arusha Declaration had warned that foreign loans would endanger Tanzanian independence. In fact, foreign aid has become vital to Tanzania, and Nyerere's policy of self-reliance and political non-alignment has helped to attract major aid donors like the World Bank whose broad aims

**Table 6.2 Tanzania's growing balance of trade problem (millions of shillings)**

| Year | Exports | Imports | Trade balance |
|------|---------|---------|---------------|
| 1965 | 1400 | 1335 | 65 |
| 1967 | 1760 | 1625 | 135 |
| 1969 | 1640 | 1659 | −19 |
| 1971 | 1777 | 2678 | −901 |
| 1973 | 2302 | 3410 | −1108 |
| 1975 | 2434 | 5424 | −2990 |
| 1977 | 4482 | 6160 | −1712 |
| 1979 | 4296 | 8941 | −4645 |
| 1981 | 5248 | 10065 | −4817 |

of promoting political stability and rural development in the Third World largely coincided with development priorities in Tanzania. But, while Tanzania still has grave economic problems after two decades of independence, there are signs of some progress towards greater social and economic equality.

**Study activity**

A standard of living index can be worked out by dividing incomes by prices paid for essential goods. Ellis carried out this exercise for rural producers in Tanzania. The results are shown in Table 6.3. Notice that the prices paid by consumers for goods bought in rural areas has

increased substantially more than the producers' prices, that is, the prices farmers obtain for their crops. In this Table, these include the main subsistence and export cash crops.

1 Draw graphs to represent the standard of living data in Table 6.3.
2 Comment on the main trends shown by each graph.
3 How do you account for the falling standard of living in Tanzania between 1969 and 1979?
4 What evidence can you find to suggest that Tanzanian development is based on the Chinese model?
5 Find out all you can about post-independence development in the neighbouring country of Kenya. Compare what you discover about Kenya with Tanzania and draw your own conclusions about the relative merits of the two development strategies. *The Financial Times* surveys are a useful source of up-to-date information on individual countries.

**Table 6.3 The standard of living in Tanzania**

| Year | Index of producers' prices | Price index of goods bought in rural areas | Standard of living index |
|------|------|------|------|
| 1969/70 | 100.0 | 100.0 | 100.0 |
| 1970/71 | 101.1 | 104.2 | 111.4 |
| 1971/72 | 104.4 | 110.4 | 104.8 |
| 1972/73 | 110.8 | 126.6 | 99.9 |
| 1973/74 | 116.3 | 152.9 | 79.4 |
| 1974/75 | 131.2 | 203.5 | 65.6 |
| 1975/76 | 198.8 | 213.2 | 84.8 |
| 1976/77 | 259.4 | 236.4 | 102.5 |
| 1977/78 | 225.5 | 264.0 | 84.0 |
| 1978/79 | 219.1 | 293.9 | 72.8 |

(1969/70 = 100).

## India

India is the ninth largest industrial nation in the world, but it has a per capita income of under $250 which is comparable to some of the world's poorest countries. The population problem – an annual increase of 15 million people,

*Figure 6.4* Modern industry in India: the Escorts Auto factory, at Faridabad

and with 320 million people living below sub-sistence level – lies at the heart of Indian poverty. India gained its independence in 1947 after a century and a half of colonial-style development under British rule.

*The Five Year Plans* Since independence, India has struggled to achieve economic and social development against a backcloth of harsh en-vironmental conditions and a rising tide of population growth. In the early 1950's the Indian government set four major long-term goals: high economic growth rates, national self-reliance, full employment and the reduc-tion of economic inequities. These national goals have been only partially realised. India has gained self-sufficiency in food grains and most industrial goods but it is still burdened with high energy costs, mass poverty and un-employment. The Indian development strategy has promoted economic growth, but it has left the issue of wealth redistribution unresolved.

The main lines of Indian development are laid down in the Five Year Plans which indicate how investment is allocated in each sector of the economy. By this method of **sectoral plan-ning** modelled on the Soviet system, develop-ment targets can be set in accordance with economic and social priorities (Table 6.4).

> **Study activity**
>
> 1 Represent the data on India's Five Year Plans in Table 6.4 on a histogram or bar graph.

> 2 What are the main trends shown on this graph?
>
> 3 Discuss the relative importance of agriculture and industry in the plans.
>
> 4 What kind of development was promoted in the Soviet Five Year Plans. Information on these Plans can be found in *A Geography of World Affairs* (Penguin Books) or regional texts on the USSR.
>
> 5 How does Indian planning differ from the Soviet model?
>
> 6 Why do you think the Soviet model appealed to the Indian government in the early 1950s?

Early priority was given to agriculture in order to boost production of food and com-modities like tea which are valuable exports. Major irrigation works were undertaken to improve farming in regions like the Punjab and West Bengal. All the Plans have set aside funds for rural development, including village indus-tries, schools and health centres. The basic transport network was expanded, particularly in the first two Five Year Plans to provide the necessary infrastructure for industrialisation which attracted heavy investment in subseq-uent plans. In an effort to diversify the pre-dominantly agricultural economy and to sub-stitute imported manufactured goods with local products, heavy industries like iron and steel, engineering and cement production were expanded. In spite of these efforts to diversify, India's exports are still dominated by a large

**Table 6.4  The allocation of funds in India's development plans since 1951 (as a percentage of the total outlay)**

| Sector | 1st Plan 1951–56 | 2nd Plan 1956–61 | 3rd Plan 1961–66 | 4th Plan 1969–74 | 5th Plan 1974–79 | 6th Plan 1979–84 |
|---|---|---|---|---|---|---|
| Agriculture and irrigation | 31 | 20 | 23 | 26 | 19 | 21 |
| Village and craft industry | 2 | 4 | 4 | 2 | 1 | 2 |
| Energy supplies | 8 | 10 | 13 | 12 | 18 | 32 |
| Industry and mining | 4 | 20 | 20 | 20 | 26 | 15 |
| Transport and communications | 26 | 28 | 20 | 20 | 18 | 14 |
| Social services | 29 | 18 | 20 | 20 | 18 | 16 |
| TOTAL | 100 | 100 | 100 | 100 | 100 | 100 |

**Table 6.5  India's leading exports in 1981**

|  | Percentage of all exports |
|---|---|
| Food and beverages | 30 |
| Tea | 6 |
| Fish products | 4 |
| Fruit and nuts | 2 |
| Coffee | 2 |
| Spices | 1 |
| Raw materials | 12 |
| Leather | 5 |
| Metal ores | 4 |
| Oilseeds | 3 |
| Manufactured products | 54 |
| Cotton goods | 7 |
| Jute goods | 4 |
| Steel | 3 |
| Chemicals | 3 |
| Tobacco | 2 |
| Others | 4 |

number of processed raw materials (Table 6.5). The development of energy supplies came to the fore after the world oil crisis when India was severely hit by escalating oil prices. India's response was to step up the search for oil, and the adoption of a nuclear energy programme; five heavy water plants had been constructed by 1984. The seventh Five Year Plan will continue to emphasize energy production with at least three more reactors and several HEP schemes. Domestic oil production, at present based on the Bombay High Field now meets 65% of the country's requirements and the target year for self-sufficiency in energy is 1990.

In general, the growth of manufacturing industry in India has been slow due to the small size of the domestic market. Outside the main urban centres like Delhi, Bombay, Madras and Calcutta, Indians still rely on traditional goods sold in village bazaars. The benefits of modern industry have gone almost entirely to the urban middle classes who are principally engaged in the modern sector of the economy. But India's plans have encouraged small-scale rural industries such as handloom textiles and brick making, and organizations like ASTRA (The Application of Science and Technology to Rural Areas) are promoting self-help schemes and the application of intermediate technology in the villages.

India's investment in social services reflects the continuing concern over poverty, malnutrition and illiteracy which are widespread in rural India and on the increase in the shanty towns or **bustees** and slums of the large cities. The long-term aim of the government is to reduce the birth rate through its official family planning programme. In spite of efforts to spread the idea and benefits of birth control, many Indians are reluctant to give up the security of large families. The traditional importance of large rural families still outweighs arguments in favour of following the family planning campaign slogan of 'we are two – we have two' (Table 6.6).

**Table 6.6  India's changing birth and death rates (per 1000 population)**

|  | 1960 | 1980 |
|---|---|---|
| Birth rate | 36 | 33 |
| Death rate | 14 | 14 |
| Rate of natural increase | 2.2% | 1.9% |

**Study activity**

India was the first country in Asia to have an official family planning campaign. Today, most Third World countries have policies for reducing population growth. Find out how some of these campaigns are promoted and what degree of success they have had in reducing fertility levels and bringing down the birth rate.

*Agricultural development* The emphasis given to agriculture in India's Five Year Plans reflects the importance of farming in the economy, accounting for a third of the country's GDP in 1983. But farming also provides a way of life for some 470 million people – 69% of the population – who live in India's half million or more villages. From being a food importing country in the 1950s, India is now self-sufficient

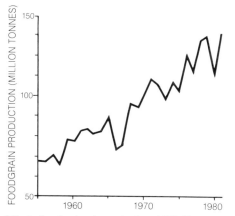

Figure 6.5    Indian foodgrain production, 1955–81

in grain although good harvests are reliant on favourable weather (Figure 6.5). Until the early 1960s, increasing food production was possible by extending the area under cultivation. But since then, high-yielding varieties of wheat and rice – the so-called miracle-seeds of the Green Revolution – have dramatically boosted crop yields under the **High Yielding Varieties Programme (HYVP)** which promotes Green Revolution farming methods. The greatest success has occurred in wheat cultivation, especially in the state of Punjab where high-yielding varieties were introduced in the 1960s together with a package of technical improvements such as irrigation, fertilizers, pesticides and mechanisation. 75% of all cultivated land in the Punjab is now irrigated compared to an average of 25% for India as a whole, and every village has supplies of electricity. Whilst wheat yields trebled, rice production rose by only 16% as the new dwarf varieties, including the famous IR-8, are vulnerable to deep flooding, pests and diseases all of which are prevalent in the humid tropical environment of southern India.

*Rural development* The Indian countryside is still beset with agrarian problems. It is dominated by small farms, fragmented holdings and tenant farmers. In 1971, 15% of all land-owning households owned 45% of India's farmland. Just over half all holdings were less

than one hectare (2.5 acres) which is regarded as the minimum farm size to maintain a family at subsistence level. **Land ceilings** legislation was introduced to limit the size of farms, but laws vary between states, and generally little has been done to limit the size of holdings under one owner, or to provide a stock of surplus land for redistribution to landless peasants, as originally intended. The widespread practice of tenancy, which was reformed in the 1960s to achieve security of tenure and fair rents, has been largely ineffectual in most rural areas. The problem of indebtedness was eased with the abolition of the rural tax collectors – the zamindars – paving the way for fairer tax collection and rural credit arrangements. Some

Figure 6.6    Average incomes in India, mid-1970s

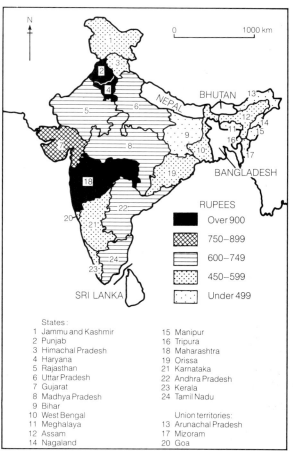

RUPEES

| | |
|---|---|
| ■ | Over 900 |
| ▨ | 750–899 |
| ▤ | 600–749 |
| ▦ | 450–599 |
| ▫ | Under 499 |

States:
1 Jammu and Kashmir
2 Punjab
3 Himachal Pradesh
4 Haryana
5 Rajasthan
6 Uttar Pradesh
7 Gujarat
8 Madhya Pradesh
9 Bihar
10 West Bengal
11 Meghalaya
12 Assam
14 Nagaland

15 Manipur
16 Tripura
18 Maharashtra
19 Orissa
21 Karnataka
22 Andhra Pradesh
23 Kerala
24 Tamil Nadu

Union territories:
13 Arunachal Pradesh
17 Mizoram
20 Goa

79

land consolidation has occurred, notably in the Punjab and Uttar Pradesh in conjunction with the HYVP making mechanisation and large-scale irrigation works more feasible. It has been estimated that India's grain production could be doubled by implementing sweeping land reforms throughout the country. Although the removal of social and economic inequities remains a major goal in India, each of the twenty two states and nine union territories can make its own decisions concerning agrarian reform. This fragmentation of responsibility for major reforms means that rural development in India is likely to be slow and piecemeal.

---

**Study questions**

1 What is the meaning of sectoral planning?
2 Why was agriculture made a priority in India's Five Year Plans?
3 How far do you think India has achieved its four long-term development goals?
4 What, in your view, are the main obstacles to development in India?
5 Describe the pattern of inequality represented by variations in average state incomes in Figure 6.6.

---

## China

China is the world's most populous country with over 1 020 million inhabitants in 1981. In spite of its huge population and numerous environmental problems, associated mainly with the monsoon climate, China has made remarkable progress along its chosen path of socialist development. When the Communist government gained power in 1949, it inherited a war-torn economy – shattered by civil conflict (1926–49) and the Japanese occupation (1939–45) – and a traditional, feudal society not much changed since the times of Confucius (c 500 BC). After three decades of communism, China has emerged as a **model of development** for Third World countries in the way it has achieved modern economic growth and reduced gross social inequities.

*Major phases of post-1949 development* Since China has a **command economy**, that is, one controlled by the State, Chinese development can only be properly understood in its political context. There have been several major shifts of policy since 1949 and Chinese development falls conveniently into four phases which reflect the changing priorities of the State.

The earliest phase coincides with the First Five Year Plan (1951–56) which was designed to rehabilitate the Chinese economy by building up the major centres of heavy industry. Over half the outlay of the First Plan went to industrialisation in an effort to make China an

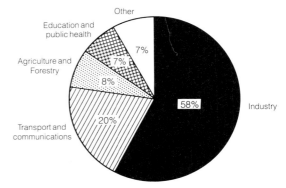

**Figure 6.7** *The main outlays in China's First Five Year Plan*

industrial nation (Figure 6.7). The Chinese received aid and technical assistance from the Soviet Union, particularly for the development of major industrial centres like Wuhan and Anshan and a new industrial site at Baotou in Nei Monggol. In 'learning from the Soviet Union', China expanded its iron and steel, coal mining, and heavy engineering industries as the foundation for a modern industrial economy. Although investment in agriculture was low, the Chinese have carried out a comprehensive programme of land reform. The new communist leaders dispossessed rich landlords of their land and redistributed it amongst poor farmers and landless peasants under the banner of 'land to the tiller'. Over a number of years the Chinese have experimented with various forms of co-operative farming which are summarized in Table 6.7. Agrarian reforms and the imple-

**Table 6.7  Summary of land reform in China**

| Period | Form of co-operation | Size and organisation |
|---|---|---|
| 1952–54 | Mutual aid teams | Private ownership of land; redistributed to poor and middle peasants; fragmented plots; mainly subsistence with surplus sold in local markets; 5–10 households work co-operatively. |
| 1955–56 | Elementary producers' co-operatives | 30–40 households in which members contribute their land, animals and tools to the co-operative. Families kept private plots for their own use; some consolidation of plots. Underemployed farm workers put on to road building and irrigation works. |
| 1957–58 | Advanced producers' co-operatives | 100–300 households with all land, equipment and livestock in collective ownership. All income derived from labour rather than value of capital contributed to collective. Most agricultural decisions made by political cadres rather than peasant farmers. |
| 1958–59 | People's communes | Variable size with an average of 4750 households organised into production teams (households) and production brigades (villages). Much regimentation of labour 'like a thousand ants gnawing at a bone'. Excessive government production targets and an outburst of iron-making in the Great Leap Forward brought disillusionment and chaos to many communes. |
| 1960– | Communes | Various changes introduced to raise productivity, diversify the rural economy with small industries and a restoration of private plots. The production brigade assumes greater importance in running agriculture. Gradual dismantling of the communes after the Cultural Revolution. |

mentation of the Eight-Point Charter (Table 6.8) have led to the consolidation of fragmented plots of land, major irrigation, flood-control and drainage systems, the efficient use of communal labour, and investment in equipment, new seeds and fertilizers. Through these measures, the Chinese have achieved nationwide food security, except in times of most severe drought.

In 1956, the Chinese inaugurated a Twelve Year Plan (1956–77) to increase agricultural production and raise living standards by en-

**Table 6.8  China's Eight Point Charter**

| | |
|---|---|
| Shui | Water conservation: irrigation and drainage |
| Fei | Fertilization: organic matter; chemical fertilizers |
| Chung | Seed selection: improved seeds; development of HYVs |
| Kung | Mechanisation: simple transplanting machines; 'walking tractors'; tractors |
| Pao | Plant production: pesticides; fungicides; insecticides |
| Nai | Close planting: greater output per area |
| Kuan | Field management: crop rotation |
| T'u | Soil conservation |

forcing the 'five guarantees' that ensure people's basic needs are met. These basic needs are defined as: having enough to eat, adequate housing and clothing, day to day necessities and a decent burial. During this phase of development the Chinese leader, Mao Tse-tung, initiated the Great Leap Forward (1958–59) to accelerate the pace of economic growth and 'overtake Britain in 15 years'. As a result, production in most industries rose dramatically as thousands of peasants gave up their normal agricultural tasks to join the ranks of factory workers. Nearly every commune had its 'backyard' blast furnaces which were constructed from brick and mud in a frenzy of activity to reach the over-ambitious targets for pig-iron production. Although targets generally were not met, and much of the iron was of very low quality, the Great Leap Forward brought an awareness of industry to millions of rural peasants, paving the way for greater industrial self-sufficiency on the communes in the 1960s. At the same time, agricultural output fell due to the shortage of labour in the fields. The food situation was further worsened by three years of prolonged droughts and severe floods (1959–61) and it appeared that China might once again live up to its historical reputation as the land of famines.

---

**Study activity**

1 The Chinese communists came to power after a long struggle against the Chinese Nationalists under Chiang Kai-shek. Why do you think communism appealed to many Chinese peasants?
2 Discuss the relevance of the Eight–Point Charter to the development of farming in China (Table 6.8).

---

In 1960, the Soviet Union withdrew its entire aid programme following the ideological break with China. This left hundreds of industrial projects incomplete and, with their agriculture in disarray after the Great Leap Forward, the Chinese switched their priorities to agriculture supported by industry. The aim of this phase of development was to encourage links between major industrial centres, such as Beijing and Shanghai, and the rural communes. The Chinese called this form of development 'walking on two legs'. The same principle was applied in farming and forestry with, for example, massive state forests being represented at the commune level by 'round the village forest belts'. New slogans appeared publicising the place of agriculture in the national economy and peasants who had deserted the communes were sent back to the countryside. The role of industry was to help agriculture become more productive by increasing the manufacture of fertilizers, farm machinery and irrigation equipment. Small workshops were set up on the communes to manufacture and repair farm machinery and peasants became involved in most aspects of production. The policy of 'walking on two legs' encouraged the development of both modern, technologically-advanced, capital-intensive industry and small-scale, labour-intensive, workshop industry using inexpensive intermediate technology.

---

**Study questions**

1 What pattern of economic growth did the Chinese expect from the Great Leap Forward?
2 How and for what reasons did China's development strategy change after 1960?
3 Explain the meaning of 'walking on two legs' in terms of Chinese development.

---

The most recent phase of development followed the period of political upheaval known as the Cultural Revolution (1966–69) when China, under Mao, turned its back on the outside world in a campaign rejecting capitalism and **revisionism** – a term used to describe a weakening of Communist principles. The Cultural Revolution caused serious economic disruption as many factories closed down and farm workers left the rural communes and migrated to the cities to attend mass meetings. The new strategy stressed industrialisation and modernisation, with the aim of turning China from being a developing country into a leading industrial nation by the year 2000. It sought to increase industrial productivity by introducing advanced technology, expanding energy production and extending the transport network. China has vast reserves of coal and aims, in its energy policy, to double production of 600 million tonnes a year by the end of the century. Coal accounts for 70% of China's energy needs and new mines are being opened each year to exploit this major natural resource. At the same time oil exploration has led to growing domestic production and the first Chinese-built nuclear reactor, near Shanghai, is expected to be completed in the 1990s. China's programme of industrialisation has boosted the value of manufactured exports, which accounted for 54% of all exports in 1981. It has also greatly expanded the number and range of consumer goods within China, reflecting the rising incomes and standards of living enjoyed by many Chinese today.

The government encouraged foreign investment by setting up four **Special Economic**

**Zones** in southern China. These special zones offered attractive tax concessions and preferential treatment for high-technology industries. Shenzhen and Zuhai, located adjacent to the colonies of Hong Kong and Macao respectively, were designated for multi-purpose economic development including industry, agriculture, trade, housing and tourism. The remaining zones at Shantou (Swatow) and Xiamen (Amoy) specialise in processing industries and tourism as both towns are historic centres.

The rigid controls imposed by the government on agriculture have been relaxed to allow more freedom for local initiatives. The so-called 'free markets' have been opened to allow farmers the opportunity to sell produce for cash and increase family incomes. Under the **responsibility system**, individual farmers or production teams may contract with the state to meet production targets in place of the fixed quota system. The communes are gradually being dismantled in favour of smaller production units based on the market town or xiang. Rural industries, animal husbandry and fish farming are being encouraged to improve both employment opportunities and diets in the countryside where some 80% of the population live. Even so, food consumption in China compares very favourably with other developing countries, standing at 2666 calories per person a day.

---

**Study questions**

Explain the significance of (a) the Special Economic Zones, and (b) the responsibility system in contemporary Chinese development.

---

*Population policies* China's huge population may be regarded as a serious obstacle to development, but China's policies on population growth have met with considerable success in reducing the birth rate through the application of strict social and economic pressures (Table 6.9). The traditional large family in China looks like a thing of the past. In the early 1960s,

**Table 6.9 China's changing birth and death rates (per 1000 population)**

|  | 1960 | 1980 |
|---|---|---|
| Birth rate | 36 | 18 |
| Death rate | 15 | 6 |
| Rate of natural increase | 3.1% | 1.2% |

China launched a massive family planning campaign in the wake of poor harvests and food shortages. Having laid the foundation of family planning through the provision of free health services and educational programmes, China now has a 'one child' policy promoted widely by slogans such as 'fewer people but higher quality'. The law forbids the marriage of women under 24 and parents may contract with the state to have one child in exchange for a range of benefits including an extra three months maternity leave on full pay, a small annual income from the government, free education and priority for a university place. Families with more than one child may lose some state benefits and may even be fined. The policy is applied less strictly in rural areas where it is recognized that labour is vital to maintain agricultural production. Many factories, however, go to some lengths to impose the rules on their workforce, publicising family details and winning state bonuses when they succeed in achieving a 100% record of one child families. This apparently harsh popul-

*Figure 6.8* A large poster in Canton reminds the Chinese that small families will help China achieve the 'four modernisations' – industry, agriculture, science and technology and military development

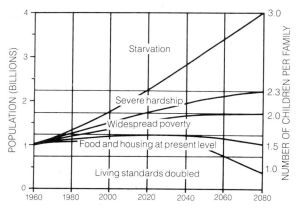

*Figure 6.9* Chinese population predictions based on family size

ation policy is designed to influence China's long-term demographic trends and to achieve a reasonable balance between population and resources, so that future generations may benefit from improved standards of living (Figure 6.9).

*Regional development* China's regional development policies have concentrated on opening up largely unexplored and under-populated areas known as **frontier regions** and multi-purpose river basin projects. Frontier regions and virgin territories, such as Xinjiang and Nei Monggol, were colonised and settled by the Chinese with large, highly mechanised **state farms** which produced grain, cotton, wool and meat. These farms also had a political role to play in providing a Chinese presence in parts of China populated mainly by national minorities. Major river basin projects are being carried out in many parts of China, but particularly on the two great rivers, the Chang Jiang and the Huang He. The most ambitious scheme is the multi-purpose plan for permanently controlling the Yellow River – the Huang He – and exploiting its water resources. Known as 'China's sorrow', the Huang He has flooded its banks more than 1500 times in recorded history with huge losses of life and damage to crops on the North China Plain. The project includes a 'staircase plan' of forty-five dams which will eventually control flood water

and prevent the removal of silt from the loess regions through which the river passes in a deep gorge. The scheme also involves extensive afforestation of badly eroded land, hillside terracing, irrigation, HEP and improved river navigation as far inland as Lanzhou. The whole plan, conceived in 1955, is expected to take fifty years to complete.

**Study questions**

1 Why do you think China's population policy is a key part of its development strategy?
2 To what extent do you think the Chinese have tackled the question of land reform more effectively than the Indians?
3 Write a short essay on the rise of the people's communes and their contribution to the development of China. Try to find additional sources of information for this question, such as Tregear's *A Geography of China*.

**Brazil**

Brazil is a striking example of a rapidly developing country with vast natural resources and great potential for economic growth. In terms of natural resources, Brazil could claim to be one of the richest countries in the world, for within its boundaries there are enormous reserves of minerals (including an estimated quarter of the world's known iron ore reserves), timber, water and agricultural land. Brazil also has a substantial population of 122 million which is growing at a rate of about 3% a year, so there is no shortage of human resources. In spite of these advantages, Brazil is confronted with severe regional problems and in recent years official development strategies have increasingly promised projects to help redress regional imbalances.

*Industrial expansion* Until recently, the Brazilian economy depended mainly on the export of coffee, rubber and cocoa, a pattern of dependence established during the colonial period before independence from Portugal in

**Table 6.10 The distribution, by sectors, of the economically active population in Brazil, 1950–80**

|  | 1950 % | 1960 % | 1970 % | 1980 % |
|---|---|---|---|---|
| Agriculture | 59.9 | 54.0 | 44.3 | 30.5 |
| Public utilities/manufacturing/construction | 14.2 | 13.2 | 18.4 | 24.9 |
| Commerce/personal services | 15.4 | 18.6 | 19.9 | 26.1 |
| Transport and communication | 4.0 | 4.6 | 4.1 | 4.2 |
| Social services/public administration/other | 6.5 | 9.6 | 13.3 | 14.3 |

**Table 6.11 Vehicle production in Brazil, 1981 (in thousand units)**

| | | |
|---|---|---|
| Volkswagen | Cars and trucks | 304.6 |
| General Motors | Cars, trucks and buses | 155.6 |
| Fiat | Cars and trucks | 133.2 |
| Ford | Cars, trucks and buses | 126.8 |
| Mercedes Benz | Trucks and buses | 49.0 |
| Toyota | Trucks | 4.0 |
| Saab-Scania | Trucks and buses | 3.5 |
| Volvo | Trucks and buses | 1.6 |

1822. By the mid-1960s the dominance of agriculture in the economy was superceded by industry, as Brazil entered the stage of economic 'take off' and emerged as one of a handful of successful newly industrialising countries in the Third World (Table 6.10). But modern economic growth became concentrated in the south-east region, and São Paulo alone has half the industrial employment of Brazil. Consequently, much of Brazil's vast territory remains undeveloped. The opening up of frontier regions like the Amazon Basin remains a major challenge for the government and the target for massive investment in the 1970s and 1980s.

Brazil laid the foundations for economic growth in its Second Plan (1956–60) which stressed the role of industry. It built up the iron and steel industry, including the large works at Volta Redonda and the new integrated steel mill near Santos, as the basis for developing related industries such as vehicle manufacture, shipbuilding and engineering. Transnational corporations, attracted by the market potential in Brazil, have had a major influence in setting up modern factories. This is exemplified by the Brazilian motor industry (Table 6.11).

From being a vehicle-importing country in 1960, Brazil now exports cars to Africa, other Latin American countries and even sends Fiats to Italy. Other industries that have expanded rapidly are cement manufacture, chemicals and light consumer industries such as textiles and footwear. The government's industrial growth policies and heavy dependence on road transport left Brazil with severe economic problems after the oil crisis in 1973. Furthermore, Brazil had initiated a long-term programme for building nine nuclear power stations with foreign loans and technical assistance. This expensive energy option, together with rising oil bills, led the Brazilian government to adopt a new energy strategy based on increasing supplies of domestic energy. The search for oil was intensified, leading to the discovery of a large oilfield off the cost of Rio de Janeiro by Petrobras, the state-controlled oil company. The government also pushed ahead with its plans to produce combustible alcohol from sugar-cane (Alcool) for use in specially converted engines. But the most spectacular energy developments have been in the expansion of HEP, with the completion of the Itaipu dam on the Parana River in 1983, at a

*Figure 6.10 Many Brazillians drive vehicles which run on alcohol fuel made from sugar-cane. By expanding the production of combustible alcohol, Brazil is able to reduce imports of oil*

cost of $14 billion. The project is shared by Brazil and Paraguay and when it is fully operational, in 1988, the turbines will generate 12.6 m kW, making it the largest in the world. Largely as a consequence of the new energy strategy, Brazil's dependence on imported oil has fallen from 45% in 1975 to 30% in 1981, although it still represents nearly half the value of all imported goods.

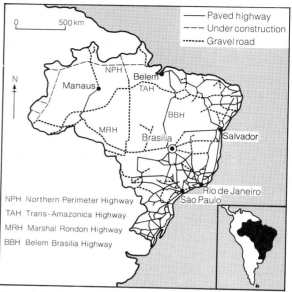

*Figure 6.11  Brazil's road network and frontier regions*

> **Study questions**
>
> 1 In what ways may Brazil be considered a resource-rich country?
> 2 Describe the two main sources of capital for Brazil's programme of industrialisation.
> 3 Using the data in Table 6.12, describe regional imbalance in Brazil. What other data would confirm this imbalance?

**Table 6.12  Population and incomes in Brazil, 1981**

| Region | Percentage of total area | Population density per km² | Percentage of total population | Percentage of national income |
|---|---|---|---|---|
| North | 42 | 1.4 | 4 | 2 |
| Central-West | 22 | 4.1 | 6 | 3 |
| South-East | 11 | 55.8 | 42 | 33 |
| North-East | 18 | 23.4 | 30 | 9 |
| South | 7 | 38.9 | 18 | 53 |

The expansion of communications has played a significant role in the development of Brazil since the first formal plan (1949–53). Although very costly, the extension of the road network was given top priority in order to tap new mineral and timber resources and to encourage colonisation in Brazil's frontier regions (Figure 6.11). The most ambitous part of the plan, and one that caught the imagination, was the Trans-Amazonica Highway. It runs from north-east Brazil across one of the world's least known and impenetrable regions, the Amazon Forest. Originally intended to help migrants leave the north-east drought zone and settle in Amazonia, the highway became a spinal route for development with feeder roads penetrating the hinterland. But

the overall benefits of the road are still unclear. On the one hand it has permitted a range of new economic activities such as mining, lumbering and farming in the Amazon region, but the exploitive character of this development is causing serious environmental damage with the destruction of the forest.

*Rural and agricultural development* Rural development and the modernisation of agriculture have been generally neglected in favour of industry and communications. Most progress has occurred in improving productivity on large, commercial farms and plantations which grow Brazil's major export crops of coffee, cocoa, sugar and soya beans. But the fundamental problems resulting from unequal patterns of land ownership, evident in the plantation or **hacienda** system inherited from the colonial period, still remain. In addition, mechanisation and the consolidation of small farms into large commercial units has increased the levels of rural unemployment and the number of landless peasant families.

These problems spill over from depressed rural areas like the north-east into major cities like Rio de Janeiro where shanty towns or

**favelas** spring up to accommodate the steady flow of migrants from the countryside. The government has sought to solve the problems of rural poverty and low agricultural productivity by opening up new land and expanding the area under cultivation, and by introducing cattle ranching on a large scale in the northern and western frontier regions of Mato Grosso, Para and Amazonia. The effect of these policies on food production has been quite significant although offset by rapid population increase. But rural poverty remains widespread and the scheme to move large numbers of families out of the overpopulated north-east region was largely unsuccessful due to hasty planning, lack of information about rain-forest environments, and inadequate technical support from agricultural specialists. Many peasants returned to their homes in the north-east, disillusioned by conditions in the Amazon Region.

*Regional policies* To some extent the responsibility for solving Brazil's acute **regional problems** has been devolved to **regional development agencies** such as SUDAM (Superintendency for the Development of Amazonas) and SUDENE (Superintendency for the Development of the North-East). These agencies supervise, co-ordinate and control **regional development strategies** to deal with specific regional problems. The north-east stands out as Brazil's most intractable problem region. It suffers from regular, prolonged droughts, high unemployment, rural poverty and an undiversified economic structure dominated by sugar production. To combat these problems, SUDENE has invested heavily in new industries and communications, and in irrigation and HEP schemes on the region's only large river, the São Francisco. New industries which have set up in the north-east can obtain tax concessions and financial help from the Regional Development Bank. The expansion of the sugar-alcohol industry has brought some economic growth to the region but SUDENE has failed to carry out much needed land reforms and it has done little to aid landless peasants and small subsistence farmers who make up the major part of the region's population. The flow of migrants from the north-east – known locally as nordestinos – continues to bear testimony to the poverty and lack of opportunity in the north-east of Brazil.

---

**Study activity**

Carry out a comparative study of problem regions in other countries and note any similarities with north-east Brazil. Possible examples are north-east England and southern Italy.

---

## South Korea

Since 1953, when South Korea emerged as a newly-independent country, it has become one of the most rapidly developing countries in the world, frequently held up as a model of development in the Third World. As a small state situated between two more powerful countries, Korea has been subjected to long periods of rule by the Chinese and, between 1910 and 1945, by the Japanese whose colonial style occupation led to developments in farming, mining and communications but little industrial or social development. American and Soviet occupation after 1945 led to the present partition of Korea into the communist Peoples' Democratic Republic of North Korea and the capitalist Republic of South Korea in the south.

---

**Study activity**

1 Find out all you can about the social and economic conditions in the Kingdom of Korea, that is, before it was annexed by Japan.
2 Make a short comparative study of the development of North and South Korea, noting in particular the way different political systems have influenced the pattern of economic and social life in the two countries. Refer to *The Financial Times* surveys of these countries and the *Handbook of World Development* published by Longmans as a guide to the Brandt Report.

---

Figure 6.12 *The agricultural sector in South Korea is efficient and highly productive as a result of rural development and modern farming methods*

**The rise of modern industry** The economic development of South Korea is a remarkable success story of industrialisation and export-oriented growth. The Koreans have achieved their long-term aim of becoming self-sufficient in food supplies and most consumer goods, and indeed are now major exporters of manufactured products. However, rapid economic growth has made South Korea heavily dependent on imported oil from the Middle East and, with large-scale borrowing from overseas to finance its programme of industrial expansion, South Korea has a huge burden of debt.

Figure 6.13 *The Hyundai Shipyards in South Korea can build ships of up to a million tonnes*

The South Korean 'economic miracle' is firmly rooted in planned industrial growth (Table 6.13). The contribution of industry to

Table 6.13 **South Korea: annual growth rates in major sectors of the economy, 1960–80**

| Sector | 1960–70 % | 1970–80 % |
|---|---|---|
| Agriculture | 4.4 | 3.2 |
| Industry | 17.2 | 15.4 |
| Services | 8.9 | 8.5 |

the South Korean GDP rose from only 6% in 1955 to 41% in 1980. Initially, South Korea adopted a programme of **import-substituting industries** such as textiles, clothing and footwear to satisfy local demand for consumer goods and to curb the rising cost of imports. These labour-intensive industries gave Korea a comparative advantage over developed countries because of the low cost of labour which allowed goods to be produced relatively cheaply. The second phase of industrialisation marked a shift away from labour-oriented production to capital-intensive, **export-led manufacturing**, and particularly to heavy industry. Using massive transfers of capital and technology from overseas, South Korea embarked on the production of iron and steel, chemicals, shipbuilding and vehicle manufacture. This phase included the development of the massive Pohang Iron and Steel Company with a capacity of 8.5 million tonnes a year, the Hyundai Motor Company which produced the first all Korean car – the Hyundai Pony – and the first of two giant dockyards which have gained South Korea an international reputation for competitiveness and efficiency (Figure 6.13). Most recently, South Korea has turned to high technology industries led by the Lucky-Goldstar Group which is expanding rapidly in the field of electronics. This trend will help to reduce the country's dependence on oil as the main source of energy – 70% of all requirements in 1980 – and also to expand its share of world markets in the lucrative electronics field currently dominated by Japan. As part of its drive to self-sufficiency, South Korea has planned an ambitious nuclear energy programme of eight reactors, due to come on stream by 1986. From very modest beginnings, South Korea has become a leading industrial country in only twenty-five years (Table 6.14).

**Table 6.14  South Korea's world ranking as an industrial nation in 1981**

| Industry | South Korea | Japan | United Kingdom | Brazil |
|---|---|---|---|---|
| Shipbuilding | 2 | 1 | 8 | 4 |
| Television sets | 4 | 1 | 6 | 7 |
| Radios | 5 | 2 | 15 | 18 |
| Cotton yarn | 7 | 4 | 24 | 25 |
| Newsprint | 11 | 3 | 16 | 21 |
| Cement | 12 | 2 | 16 | 8 |
| Steel | 18 | 3 | 16 | 12 |
| Vehicles | 14 | 1 | 7 | 10 |

**Study questions**

1 Analyse the trends indicated by the data in Table 6.15.
2 How far is it possible to detect major phases in the development of manufacturing industry in South Korea from this data?

**Table 6.15  South Korea: changes in the pattern of exports, 1978–83**

| | Percentage of all exports 1978 | 1983 |
|---|---|---|
| All manufactured goods | 88.7 | 94.4 |
| Light manufactured goods | 53.6 | 39.6 |
| (Textiles) | (31.6) | (25.0) |
| Heavy manufactured goods | 26.4 | 42.4 |
| (Iron and Steel) | (4.3) | (10.2) |
| (Ships) | (6.3) | (15.4) |
| Electronic goods | 8.7 | 12.5 |
| All non-manufactured goods | 11.3 | 5.6 |

*Rural and social policies*  South Korea also has an impressive record of achievement in agriculture having reached the target of self-

sufficiency in food set in the 1962–66 Five Year Plan. South Korean farms are amongst the most highly productive in Asia due to the widespread use of 'Green Revolution' farming practices on efficient owner-occupied farms. The decline in the agricultural workforce from 66% in 1960 to 34% in 1980 is a measure of the trend towards farm efficiency and mechanisation. Rural development programmes are promoted by broadcasting, films, instructional literature and farm advisors.

Farmers are also supported by the Saemaul Undong or New Community Movement, which has a network of over 30000 clubs. The clubs help spread government farm policies and ideas, and improve incomes which fall well below the levels in urban areas. The main policies aim to increase farm productivity, develop small and medium-sized rural industries to help diversify the rural economy, and to improve South Korean farming in both technology and management.

The introduction of population control policies has made an important contribution towards rapid social and economic progress in South Korea. The rate of population increase has fallen from 2.6% in the 1960s to 1.8% in the early 1980s thus reducing the pressure of population on resources. This demographic trend has been accompanied by rapid urbanisation and the phenomenal growth of the capital city, Seoul, from a million inhabitants in 1950 to 8.5 millions in 1981, mainly as a result of rural–urban migration. Nearly a quarter of all South Koreans now live in the capital and a further 30% of the population is classed as urban.

**Study questions**

1 Using the appropriate data on South Korea from the Table on page 14, justify the claims that South Korea is (a) a middle income country; (b) a newly industrialising country; (c) a very rapidly developing country.
2 Summarise the main reasons for the 'economic miracle' in South Korea.

## Conclusion

The case studies described in this section raise a number of important questions about the nature and purpose of development. For example, does rapid economic growth necessarily become translated into better welfare and living conditions for the population as a whole? Is a centrally-planned state more efficient in dealing with the fundamental problems of underdevelopment than a democratic, capitalist one? Is it possible or even desirable for the world's least developed countries to achieve self-reliance and social equality without first creating a healthy, growing economy?

The evidence presented in the two studies of newly-industrialising countries suggests that rapid economic growth only brings gains in human welfare if the government actively pursues a policy of wealth redistribution. The Brazilian 'economic miracle' has been achieved at a price which includes widespread urban and rural poverty, growing unemployment, land-lessness amongst peasant farmers and the proliferation of sub-standard housing in shanty towns. South Korea, on the other hand, has combined remarkable economic growth through industrialisation with a reduction in social inequality. The government has taken measures to ensure that the rural population shares in the country's economic prosperity by promoting modern farming methods and rural development.

The most effective policies for reducing social inequality and promoting national self-reliance have occurred in centrally-planned states of which China is an outstanding example. By tackling the basic problem of underdevelopment through predominantly state-run industries and collectively-organised agriculture, China has moved further towards social equality than most Third World countries. In contrast to India which has only paid lip-service to wealth redistribution, China has put its egalitarian ideology into practice by persuading the bulk of population to implement it. Thus China has begun to solve some of its deep-rooted problems, like population growth, through practical measures while India tends to make statements of intent without putting them into practice. In welfare development and the provision of basic needs, the Chinese have succeeded using mass self-help schemes like the 'barefoot doctor' service, with the result that the Chinese peasant is materially better off than his Indian counterpart who has not had the benefit of similar schemes.

Many Third World countries aim to achieve self-reliance and independence from economic domination by developed countries. By adopting a socialist development strategy, Tanzania has reduced economic differentials, particularly between urban and rural communities, and has provided basic welfare needs in many of its villages. But economic growth has been very slow, so to achieve its goals of socialism and self-reliance, Tanzania has become a major recipient of foreign aid and increasingly dependent on other countries. The obstacles to economic growth in very poor countries like Tanzania are severe, and future development is likely to require support from aid programmes for a long time to come.

---

**Revision**

1 Summarise the main differences between the Indian and Chinese development strategies.
2 To what extent do the case studies suggest that rapid population growth is a major obstacle to development?
3 What common development goals, if any, do the countries described in this chapter share?
4 How far do you think a development strategy such as the Chinese one may be transferable to another country?

# 7

# Global problems and prospects

The idea of spaceship earth was introduced at the beginning of this book to draw attention to the great debate concerning the earth's carrying capacity and the fragile balance between population, resources and the environment. Subsequent chapters investigated the processes of social and economic development and the varying degrees to which people and countries in different parts of the world have achieved material and personal well-being.

## People and the environment

The majority of countries in the Third World are striving for economic growth so that they may have a fairer share of the world's wealth. How far they are or will be able to succeed depends largely on whether the physical and social possibilities for growth outweight the limitations. The fundamental elements in this equation are the supply of physical resources for development such as land for agriculture, minerals and sources of energy, and population growth which ultimately depends upon these resources for its survival.

There are signs that, at least for some regions, the race between the supply of resources and the growth of population is already lost. In north-east Africa, especially in Ethiopia, Somalia and Uganda, an estimated eight million people are seriously at risk from starvation. This catastrophic situation was caused by overpopulation, war and civil strife and a prolonged drought which drastically reduced crops and supplies of food, forcing thousands of people away from their homes. In the Karamoja District of Uganda alone, some 400 to 500 people were dying each day at the height of the drought in 1980. It appears that here, at least, the **physical limits to growth** have been reached.

In this region and in the Sahel, help has come from the developed countries. Between 1975 and 1980, £4000 million of aid was poured into this devastated part of Africa to assist in reversing the effects of desertification. The world development and environment agency, Earthscan, reports that plans and hopes to save the region are now fading owing to the size of the problem, political uncertainty, lack of co-operation between relief agencies and their inability to organize development projects effectively. Any further economic progress is very unlikely because of these **social limits to growth.**

Another part of the limits to growth equation is man's ingenuity and ability to overcome many problems via technical innovation. In the heart of the Sahel, a regional solar energy centre has been set up, with the assistance of the EEC, to provide Mali with renewable supplies of energy using photovoltaic cells to produce cheap electricity. This technical achievement will provide power for pumps to draw water from deep wells for villages in a region that traditionally relies on human and animal power and on shallow wells which quickly dry up.

What, then, will be the future pattern of global development? Will it be one of impending disaster, with growing population problems, misery and ecocatastrophe as indicated by recent events in parts of Africa? Or will it be one of steady economic growth prompted by technical achievements, controlled population growth and resource transfers to the poorest countries in the Third World? There are no straightforward answers to questions like these about the great debate on future worlds, but some light has been shed on the issues by a number of global models which try to predict future patterns of world development.

### Study activity

1 Discuss the information provided in Figure 7.1 which is taken from *The State of the Environment.*
2 Why should the state of the environment provide valuable indications of the balance between supply and demand in the development equation?

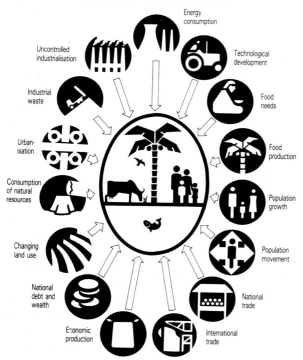

*Figure 7.1   Major influences on the environment*

Energy consumption

Uncontrolled industrialisation

Technological development

Industrial waste

Food needs

Urbanisation

Food production

Consumption of natural resources

Population growth

Changing land use

Population movement

National debt and wealth

National trade

Economic production

International trade

## Optimistic models

The most optimistic forecasts have come from the Hudson Institute in the USA under Herman Kahn. In the scenario of world development described in *The Year 2000* (1967), Kahn predicted that economic growth would continue unabated for the next 30 years and that all countries would become generally wealthier although the gap between rich and poor countries would remain. The model assumes that technological improvements will overcome resource deficiencies, but events in the early 1970s, particularly the oil crisis and the widening development gap forced Kahn to reassess the model. In *The Next 200 Years* (1976), Kahn's team produced a new model in which economic growth slows down but more than two thirds of the world will have a GNP per capita over $1 000. The basis of this prediction is the **demographic transition** and accelerated economic growth per capita in the Third World. As Third World countries move through the demographic transition from high to low and eventually to zero population growth rates, the pressure of population on resources will recede so that more wealth is available per person. The model leaves the question of how wealth is to be redistributed from its present unequal pattern largely unanswered. It also ignores many of the environmental problems that accompany rapid economic growth, such as pollution, and so as a model of world development it is very limited.

## The limits to growth

In 1972 a computer model of the world was described in a best-selling book called *The Limits to Growth.* The aim of the model was to warn of a potential world crisis by putting forward a doomsday scenario for the year 2100. The five major elements which give rise to the impending global disaster predicted by Meadows in the Limits to Growth model are summarized in Figure 7.2.

The basic assumption in the model is that

Figure 7.2   The limits to growth in the world model

each of these elements, such as deteriorating environmental quality as measured by pollution levels, is changing at an accelerating rate known as **exponential growth**. The model itself is a complex series of computerised predictions in which trends may be altered by adjusting the data that is fed into the system. The standard world model is based on historical trends between 1900 and 1970 (Figure 7.3). It assumes there are no major changes in the supply of resources, levels of industrialisation and population growth rates until the point at which exponential growth leads to rapidly diminishing resources, reduced industrial output, increased pollution followed by falling population. If restrictions are placed on population growth and industrialisation, the two elements that principally cause resource exhaustion and pollution, then it might be

Figure 7.3   The Limits to Growth Standard Run model

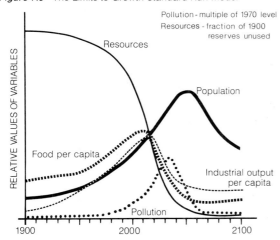

possible to achieve what Meadows called a stabilised world model in which the global system is in a **state of equilibrium** (Figure 7.4).

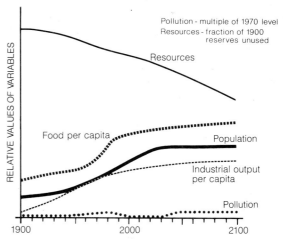

Figure 7.4   The Limits to Stabilised Growth World 2 model

A number of factors could upset the gloomy forecasts made in *The Limits to Growth*. There are as yet undiscovered sources of raw materials and there is also the probability of technological breakthroughs which will permit the more efficient use of resources and even the formulation of new ones. There are ways of controlling and reducing levels of pollution, provided governments are prepared to pay for the research and technology. The birth rate has been lowered in some parts of the Third World so unlimited population growth continuing until the Malthusian checks finally set in – famine, war, disease and pestilence – can be prevented. The Science Policy Research Unit (SPRU) in Britain took the 'limits' computer programme and gave it more optimistic data. By changing the assumptions in this way, the world model is dramatically altered (Figure 7.5). Now the year 2100 may experience economic growth instead of catastrophe. However interesting – or frightening – these models may be, they are only as good as the data on which they are based. They cannot, for example, look at the way different social systems operate or how different sets of values will be translated into development. And it is far

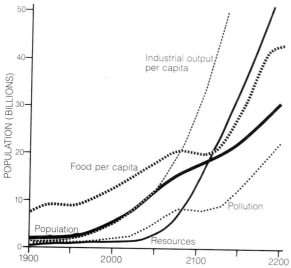

*Figure 7.5* *The World 3 model with changed resource, pollution, agricultural and capital distribution assumptions*

from certain that all the developing countries will follow the materialistic development path of the western capitalist world.

---

**Study questions**

1 Why is the Limits to Growth model described as pessimistic?
2 How far do you think the gloomy forecasts are realistic?

---

## The world in the year 2000

What will the world be like in the twenty-first century? Whether the growth or doomsday

*Figure 7.6* *Global issues in the year 2000*

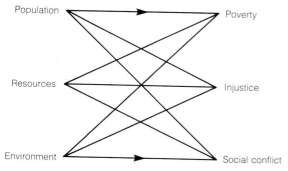

scenarios of development are accurate in their predictions, it will be different. According to *Global 2000*, a study initiated by President Carter in 1977, the world will be faced with two major sets of inter-related problems (Figure 7.6).

The forecasts made in *Global 2000* and summarised below, are bleak (Table 7.1). The consequence of the major trends is increased poverty, injustice and social conflict as the gap

---

**Table 7.1    Prospects for the world in the year 2000**

1  The world's population will grow from 4 billion in 1975 to 6.35 billion. The rate of increase will slow down marginally from 1.8% to 1.7% a year. 90% of the world's population growth will occur in the Third World.
2  Third World Economies (GDPs) are expected to expand more rapidly than those in the developed countries, but GDP per capitas will remain low and the wealth gap between DCs and LDCs will increase.
3  World food production is predicted to increase by 90% – 3% a year – although this translates into a per capita increase of less than 15% or 0.5% a year. The bulk of the food increases will occur in the DCs and food consumption in LDCs is expected to decrease.
4  During the 1990s, world oil production will approach geological estimates of maximum production capacity. Needs for fuelwood in LDCs will exceed available supplies by about 25%.
5  Non-mineral resources appear sufficient to meet projected demand bur further discoveries and investments will be needed to maintain reserves.
6  Regional water shortages will become severe. Population growth alone will cause water requirements to double in the Third World and still greater increases are needed to improve standards of living in LDCs.
7  Significant losses of world forests will continue as demand for timber increases. Some 40% of the existing forest cover will disappear.
8  Serious deterioration of soils will occur worldwide due to erosion, loss of fertility, desertification, salinisation and waterlogging.
9  Atmospheric pollution, including concentrations of carbon dioxide, will increase and acid rain caused by increased fuel combustion will damage rivers, lakes, soils and plant life.
10 Rapid urban growth in LDCs will put extreme pressures on sanitation, water supplies, health care, food, shelter and jobs. Many cities will become inconceivably large. Uncontrolled (shanty town) settlements will proliferate.

between the haves and have nots widens, not only between the countries of the North and South, but within countries in the form of regional and social inequality.

The *Global 2000* report suggests that these trends and predictions are not irreversible given wise policies on family planning, soil conservation, reafforestation, pollution control and a more equitable division of resources between the countries and peoples of the world. For the Brandt Commission, reporting on its investigations into international development issues in 1980, the major global issue was the global pattern of inequality between North and South. Brandt's recommendations were aimed at achieving a **new international economic order** in which the world's poorest countries are given greater assistance to participate as equal partners in, for example, international trade. Global models such as the Limits to Growth warn that prosperity on the scale reached by most developed countries will never be attainable in much of the Third World since the earth's capacity to sustain economic growth is limited and already under stress. The great debate on future worlds will continue as new models are devised and man's ability to predict becomes increasingly refined. Geographers, too, will continue to contribute towards the debate and offer practical solutions to development through their study and understanding of the earth as the home of people.

# Acknowledgements

The author and publishers would like to thank the following for permission to reproduce illustrations and photographs.

Dr S Buczacki (B & B Photographs) 6.12
Camerapix-Hutchison 2.6, 6.10
FAO 5.3
Trevor Humphries; *Financial Times* 6.4
Format 3.3, 4.8
Richard and Sally Greenhill 6.8
Korea National Tourism Corporation 6.13
Occidor 5.1
Andrew Reed 4.12
Richard Willson; *South* 5.10
*The State of the Environment*, UNEP, 1984
Tropix 6.2

References are made within the text to certain publications as sources of information and further reading. The publishers of these publications include Longman Publishers Ltd, Oxford University Press, Pan Books Ltd, Scientific American.

Acknowledgements are also due to the following sources from which illustrations have been adapted.

Dr Arno Peters
Hobsbawm, E J *Industry and Empire*, Weidenfeld & Nicolson Ltd, 1968
International Tea Committees, London
Lamprey, H *Integrated Project on Arid Lands,* Pluto Press
*State of the World Atlas*, Pan
United Nations Conference on Desertification, 1977
World Bank

# Index